The Sound of Water, The Sound of Wind

and other early works by a Mountain Monk

The Sound of Water, The Sound of Wind

and other early works by a Mountain Monk

Zen Master Bopjong

Translated from the Korean and Edited by

Brian Barry

Jain Publishing Company
Fremont, California
jainpub.com

Jain Publishing Company, Inc. is a diversified publisher of college textbooks and supplements, as well as professional and scholarly references, and books for the general reader. A complete, up-to-date listing of all the books, with cover images, descriptions, review excerpts, specifications and prices is always available on-line at **jainpub.com**. Our booksPLUS® division provides custom publishing and related services in print as well as electronic formats., and our learn24x7® division provides e-learning related products and services.

Copyright © 2010 by Master Bopjong. All rights reserved. No part of this book may be reproduced, stored in a retrieval system, or transmitted, in any form or by any means, electronic, mechanical, photocopying, recording or otherwise, without the written permission of the publisher except for brief passages quoted in a review.

Acknowledgement is made to Korea Literature Translation Institute (LTI Korea) for financial assistance in the production of this book.

ISBN 978-0-89581-825-6
Printed in the United States of America

CONTENTS

Part I: Branches Snapping in the Snow

CONTENTS *(continued)*

Part II: What More Could You Want?

CONTENTS *(continued)*

PART III: THE SOUND OF WATER, THE SOUND OF WIND

Introduction by the Translator

In addition to being Korean Buddhism's most prolific modern essayist, Zen (Korean: Seon) Master Bopjong is one of Korea's most outstanding, respected, and popular writers. For decades his books have reached the best-seller list, staying there for months at a time. One major reason is that Master Bopjong has a deep, abiding love for his heritage and for expressing his native language. In addition, his ability to express the purity of Korean sentiment makes him beloved by a full spectrum of the populace. He has also won the respect of the general public by leading an exemplary monastic life free from the fetters and confinements of materialism.

Master Bopjong is much more than a writer. He is also an educator and a spiritual guide. Through his countless writings since the 1960s, he has taught the public much about Buddhist thought, teachings, and morality. Simultaneously he has provided numerous insights into monastic life and how to make progress along the Buddhist path. In the process, he has also given value and direction to countless people of all ages.

Although Ch'an was first introduced from China to Korea during the Unified Silla kingdom (668-937CE), it did not take firm root until the ensuing Goryeo dynasty (918-1392). Goryeo gave birth to a number of highly important masters who stand today as pillars of Korean Seon. During the following Joseon dynasty (1392-1910), Buddhism was officially repressed in favor of Confucianism, and temples were driven from the cities to the countryside. This proved to be fortuitous for preserving Korea's outstanding Seon traditions in mountain temple environments, and they remain today as the backbone of Korean Buddhism. The ancient Chinese Ch'an traditions have been preserved, molded into Korean form, and transmitted to a degree unmatched in other countries. It is from this great tradition that Master Bopjong expresses himself.

Master Bopjong entered monastic life on Korea's southeast coast in 1955, shortly after the end of the Korean War. As is tradition, he spent his early years training in many Seon meditation temples. Eventually he moved to Bongeunsa Temple in southern Seoul, which was still very much countryside at the time, but a countryside that was about to be dramatically transformed beyond recognition. After he spent a few years there, the rapidly sprawling city began encroaching on the area, and the distant mountains beckoned him back. He retreated to a hermitage, Buril-am, near Songgwangsa Temple, Korea's third Jewel Temple representing the Sangha (Buddhist community), in Korea's southwest. Songgwangsa is historically renowned as Korea's most eminent meditation temple, having produced a series of major National masters during the Goryeo dynasty. After several years at Buril-am, however, Master Bopjong moved on again, this time because, due to his growing reputation, people, not the city, were encroaching on him and his practice.

Increased fame and recognition had become burdensome to a spirit searching for clarity and simplicity, so Master Bopjong foraged deeper into the mountains where he could remain aloof from the world of din and dust, immerse himself in his search, and continue to write of his insights and experiences. The title of his first book, in 1976, *Musoyu* (Possessionless), has enduringly typified his quest to live a pure, uncontaminated life of simplicity. This approach to life became the fuel for his future works and for his reputation as a true practitioner. He continues to live, practice, and write in an undisclosed location deep in the towering mountains of Gangwon Province far to the east of Seoul.

Through his writings, Master Bopjong stresses a number of themes he considers conducive to a happy existence. "Possessionless" is one of his favorite expressions but not always one to take literally. While in absolute terms we are all possessionless when we come into this world and when we leave it as well, he also uses the term to express an approach to life in which people possess and use only what is necessary—frugality. If one of anything is all that one really needs, even a ballpoint pen, then there's no need for multiples. Another of his favorite expressions in later works is *chongbin*, the equivalent of "honorable poverty" or, more figuratively, "decent simplicity"—a clean, no-frills existence. In addition, nonattachment to what we do have is another important meaning of "possessionless." Master Bopjong summarizes in a quote from a later book: "The secret to happiness is not to be found in how much we have of what we need, but in how free we are from what we don't need."

Additionally, through these works, you may come to appreciate the importance that Master Bopjong gives to both microscopic and macroscopic mindfulness. Rather than writing about koans (Korean: hwadu), he teaches the importance of steadfast observation and total awareness of oneself and of one's surroundings as essential to the process of cleansing the heart. Zen's "beginner's mind," empathy and compassion for all forms of life, freedom from confining attachments, and the wisdom of blossoming anew everyday are additional Buddhist themes that we can easily find throughout Master Bopjong's writings. Additionally, even in many of his early works, he demonstrated a great concern, through his Buddhist training, for the environment at a time when Korea was rushing on with industrialization, a time when concern for the environment was not only unheard-of but even unthinkable.

While many of Master Bopjong's essay collections include rather sharp observations of Korean social and political phenomena over the decades, I have chosen to limit the selection here to more universal themes that should appeal to a much broader audience. The works in this collection are from five of Master Bopjong's early publications: *Musoyu* (Possessionless), 1976; *Seo inneun saramdeul* (People Standing Everywhere), 1978; *Yeonghon ui moeum* (From the Soul), 1983; *Sanbang handam* (Leisurely Chats in the Mountains), 1983; and *Mulsori baramsori* (The Sound of Water, The Sound of Wind), 1986. After much consideration, I have kept the articles in chronological order rather than categorizing them by theme. By doing so, I hope to provide the reader with the added interest of watching Master Bopjong's mentality, practice, and depth of perception develop over the early decades.

I'd like to ask readers to take their time with this collection. The essays are simple and expressive, but there is plenty to munch on hidden within each one. So you may find the book much more enjoyable and meaningful by reading only a limited number of essays at a time, and perhaps even rereading each in a day or two, and perhaps again in the future. Also, you may find the contents more enjoyable by ruminating here and there and reading, rather than in order, each essay as it strikes your fancy. Let your intuition guide you. It is in this way, too, that you may more easily catch the overriding flavor of Master Bopjong's contributions to Korean and Seon literature and thought. And I hope that, like the traditional and magical Korean *ondol* (warm rock) hypocaust radiant heating system that gradually warms the floor, the flavor of his writings will slowly but surely warm your spirit.

For this collection, I express my sincere gratitude to the Korean Literature Translation Institute for its support for the completed translation. My special thanks also go to Kim Jeong-Ho, a long-time co-worker and friend, for his valuable advice in working through the more ethereal parts of some essays. I also extend this gratitude to Mr. Mukesh Jain of Jain Publishing Co. for his kindness and patience in bringing the manuscript to publication, and to Ms. Marilyn Silverman for her excellent proofreading.

In the Buddhist tradition, I dedicate this work to the happiness and well-being of all sentient beings. And may you enjoy this small anthology of Master Bopjong's early works!

Brian Barry
Seoul

Part I:

Branches Snapping in the Snow

1. Wandering Trees

Trees are supposed to be planted in the earth, not in the air. Yet there are trees today that are standing on gray sidewalks and withering away, unable to find their real homes.

When spring arrives it's easy to spot alleys filled with gardeners' carts and A-frames lined up and loaded with rows of brilliant plants and trees and flowers. Of course there is a tinge of sadness in realizing that all of these were uprooted out of their original homes, but from an optimistic perspective, we can think of them as heading for healthy new homes in healthy new earth.

We all know that normally the season for transplanting is spring, before new buds sprout. We also know that it is during this season that even withered branches can be stuck in the ground and then blossom, and that lilacs can bloom out of seemingly dead soil. That's the power of the life force of spring.

But it's times like right now, when spring turns into summer, that the nearly rootless sidewalk trees in the cities are doing no more than loitering around in dust and noise. Trees without their own soil look bleak and lonesome. Trees with pallid flowers loaded on carts and A-frames look pathetic. The ends of the branches exude the weariness and melancholy of a wanderer who left home a long time ago. With just a little imagination, one can practically hear the low moans of the trees, as the sun fades into a haze, asking, "Isn't there a place for me?"

It's also in the springtime that runaway kids come to the mountain temples, and their number increases as society becomes more complex and life becomes more complicated. A lot of the youngsters are dropouts. It's as if they're about to give up even before giving life a try. Has the world really become so harsh and defiled that it drains their lively, youthful spirits?

It's with a heavy heart that we eventually send them back to the secular world. Life is not a happy one for people who, unable to find their proper place, spend it buried in banality and boredom; yet, it's an even sadder commentary that youths, at a time in their lives when they should be filled with liveliness and passion and joy, have to resort to seeking out temples in the mountains. We have to seriously consider what society can do about this. The young trees that haven't found their own earth yet are still wandering and wilting in the dust and noise of the city streets. *(1965)*

2. Boxing Matches

If we had our own "Constitution for Humanity," it would naturally state that love is higher than hate, understanding is greater than anger, and peace is more precious than war.

We still have scars left over from the Korean War, bloody memories that can neither be forgotten nor rinsed away. On June 25, 1950, an unforgivable struggle between brethren broke out on the Korean Peninsula.

Coincidently, on June 25 of this year, fists were again flying under a roof in Seoul: The World Junior Middleweight Boxing Championship was taking place. On this day soldiers on leave, civil servants, and other citizens were more concerned with those flying fists than they were about the memories of the ravages and scars of war. To most people the admission price—equivalent to six sacks of barley—would have been well worth it to watch the event in person.

Nowadays, there are frequent wrestling and boxing matches held under that same gymnasium roof and no doubt in gymnasiums around the world. And at each event warmongers fight their way into the gymnasium to get a seat. But sometimes these fans take their patriotism too far, screaming "Trample him!" "Kill him!" and the like, even throwing their seats, rocks or empty bottles into the ring. Their side has to win and the opponent has to be trampled and annihilated, simply because he is the opponent.

So long as this type of "patriotism" exists in the hearts of humanity, there will be no end to the stench of chemical warfare and slaughter around the world, because a hating heart is the spark that ignites wars.

Do hating and beating others come from a paragraph in that "Constitution for Humanity"?

At a time when voices screaming for humaneness are becoming hoarse, the cruelty of boxing and wrestling, under the guise of fair-and-square sporting performances, is nothing more than a disgrace.

Isn't cheering at the sight of another human bleeding in a gymnasium a bit reminiscent of the Roman Coliseum? *(1966)*

3. Meetings

Birth is certainly a natural, even mechanical process in the animal kingdom, and it is only through interaction that we grow and form as true humans. The maturation process is a continuous one that ripens through meetings, through books, through travel to different places, and through thought systems.

A meeting carries with it the meaning of opening our eyes, of being able to see new worlds that previously were not open to us. As a result, through meetings, new life shoots forth from within us. It's then that we begin to get a feel for the meaning of life.

Once there was a man who fought his way through a blizzard to meet a teacher. And once he arrived, he stood outside the teacher's room all-night long getting half buried in the snow. The next day, in front of the unresponsive teacher's room, he cut off one of his hands. He was willing to give up not only his body but even his life for the Dharma. And this is how Shenkuang became a disciple of Bodhidharma. The man was capable of being born again only by abandoning himself. Through meetings, sometimes we have to suffer the pain of self-abandonment in order to grow, which is what Shenkuang did. He went on to become the Second Patriarch of Ch'an as Master Huik'e, the Dharma name that Bodhidharma had given him.

Again today, as everyday, the poetic city streets bustle with people on their way to meet others. However, if the joy of life and a sense of gratitude are missing, it's not a genuine meeting: at best, it's a form of socializing, and at worst, it's more of a collision. In a true meeting, there has to be a somber attitude of searching for truth.

"Who am I? How should I live?"

It's only when you are lost in the search to answer these questions that a true meeting with yourself can take place, by staying up night after night until your vision brightens. And then you may meet your true self and you'll never be alone again. Your heart beats with the joy of replacing the pain of loneliness of the small self with the all-inclusive Self, and you become much, much clearer and much, much deeper.

People can't become fully human on their own. We can grow as humans only through genuine meetings.

It's spring, a time of hope, a time when we ought to meet something new.

A time when we should open up new eyes. *(1967)*

4. Buddhas Move

One of the most impressive scenes from the life of the Buddha is his first Dharma talk, the "first turning of the wheel" at the Deer Park in Benares. The Buddha walked there, all 250 kilometers, from Bodhgaya, the place of his enlightenment. Of course in those days there were no means of transportation, and the Buddha walked barefoot and alone through the sweltering heat of the summer. He walked to Benares because he wanted to teach his former companions, five ascetics, the path to opening the Eye.

He was unable to resist going. He could not stay put under the Bo tree where he had become enlightened. He had to go to Benares because that was his compassionate nature: He wanted to teach his former companions.

At the time, the Buddha dropped the language of the Brahmans in favor of the common language of the region so that he could communicate with ordinary people. Wherever he went throughout his life he talked in a way that his audience could understand. And since he taught simply and compassionately and wisely, those who listened to him joyfully opened their hearts to him.

The Buddha was born on the road and he spent his life on the road. And he finally passed into nirvana on the road. He was an engaged Buddha with the mission of an awakened being, and as such he did not rest a single day. Until the moment he passed into nirvana, he was still, at the age of eighty, the same teacher of the Dharma to all as he had been when he had walked to Benares at the age of thirty-five. He was an active, moving Buddha. He was not a statue-like Buddha who sat quietly waiting for offerings to come to him. *(1967)*

5. Branches Snapping in the Snow

One late afternoon around sunset, a longhaired student showed up at the hovel of an elderly mountain monk. He looked rather nervous as he pulled out a letter written by his father, a close friend of the monk.

The student had been tossed out of school and the father had sent him to the monk with a request to try to straighten the boy out. Having read the letter, the elderly monk didn't say a word. He went out into the back yard. The boy just sat there.

After a while, the monk returned with a rather late supper that he offered the boy. Then the monk poured some warm water into a wash-basin and told the boy to wash his feet. Suddenly, tears started to stream down the boy's face. He had expected to get yet another reprimand, this time from the monk. But instead, the monk didn't say a word. He simply waited on the boy. The monk had correctly perceived that the boy had suffered enough scolding and that what he really needed, even more than a thousand nice words, was a bit of tender care.

Mountain people know that during the winter many trees lose their branches. The branches on big, thick pines that stubbornly withstood the onslaught of violent summer storms suddenly fall to the ground under the weight of a mantle of snow. As the gently falling flakes settle and accumulate on the branches, they eventually bring the branches down. By the end of winter, from a distance the mountains look as haggard and emaciated as sickly faces.

It's impossible to get to sleep nights when surrounding valleys echo with the sound of branches snapping in the snow. Perhaps that's because the sound leads one to dwell on the implications of the tough and sturdy being overcome by the gentle.

It was not through his supernatural powers, nor through his dignity, nor through his authority that the Buddha Sakyamuni turned the serial slayer Angulimala into a monk. He did it the only way possible, through compassion. Even the worst mass murderer cannot resist the warmth of unconditional love.

The smooth, round, pretty pebbles at the seashore became that way from the gentle caresses of the waves, not from being smashed to pieces by a blunt instrument. *(1968)*

6. Namu Amitabul

Namu Amitabul (Amitabha) is a chant that is familiar to Koreans in all walks of life. Sometimes, however, I can't help feel a tinge of remorse when I realize how casually it is used and how many people have a complete misconception of its real meaning. There are plenty of Buddhists and non-Buddhists alike who use it much the same way as Christians may invoke the expression, "Oh, Lord!"

Namu is the informal Korean pronunciation of the Sanskrit Namo or Namas and it has the meaning of going to, seeking, taking refuge in. Amitabul comes from Amitayus and Amitabha, meaning "Buddha of Infinite Life" and "Buddha of Infinite Light," respectively. According to the sutras, Amitabha is the Buddha of the Western Paradise which is supposedly more than ten trillion lands to the west. People who wish to be reborn there are told to fervently chant Namu Amitabul—"I take refuge in Amitabha."

However, we should take into consideration the Buddha's very skillful use of expedients to make things comprehensible to the audience he was addressing. It's a bit difficult to image that "more than ten trillion lands to the west" should be taken literally.

Consider this: "Mind is Buddha, and if you have a pure mind, wherever you are is the Pureland." Such a direct teaching as this affirms for us that Buddhism clearly is focused on present reality, the here and now.

"Infinite life," or eternal life, is a metaphor for compassion, and "infinite light" is a metaphor for wisdom. Compassion and wisdom, the twin pillars of Buddhism, are to be found in our hearts, not in some distant land. So Namu Amitabul is not a mantra to be recited over and over to get you into a Paradise some ten trillion lands to the west after you die. It is a chant to bring the best of compassion and wisdom out of us so that we may live compassionately and wisely in this life.

In a world where we all live so closely together and where life is so complicated, religious people who try to transcend the here and now—regardless of where they are and what they are doing—threaten the very existence of that religion. If we as monks do not bestow compassion and wisdom on the populace right here and right now and instead turn to selfish interests and pursuits, then there is no possible way to become infinite life and infinite light. Our actions have to match our words. *(1968)*

7. Being Together

They call autumn the season of parting. And perhaps that's why people seem to get together more during the fall. A fall wedding in the family is the perfect excuse to renew old acquaintances and the wedding halls are bursting with invited guests. The head monk at our temple will officiate this fall at a number of weddings for those who can't afford a regular secular ceremony, and no doubt there'll be lots of guests coming to the temple.

It's interesting to listen to various opinions about marriage. Some people are a bit bitter about it, as if it were an unavoidable punishment that they must submit to during this lifetime. Some talk like anthropologists about the necessity of propagating the species. Then there are the good-natured conformists who just get married because everybody else does.

A certain young woman whom I hadn't seen around for a while suddenly appeared at the temple a few days ago. She was much more talkative than she had been before and she said that she was going to get married this fall. I kind of jokingly asked her why, since she had always said that she would never get married. She replied that she had met someone she really liked and wanted to be with all the time. She proceeded to tell me all about him.

She was both naive and sincere in her love and in her desire to be with him, so I wished her the best of luck.

It has always been true that when people in love can't be together, it's like having a shadow of gloom cast over them.

But wishing to be together can't be anything more than a kind of hope. The basic nature of the human being is to be alone. We are born alone and we die alone. As we live our lives, there's the problem of inevitably being alone no matter how many people live with us, just as each tree in the forest stands by itself. One doesn't have to borrow the words of a poet to envision each one of us dragging our shadow along the horizon.

Since we all have different karma, we all have different ideas and behavior. Following the laws of karma, we come together and when the karma is over we go our separate ways. And of course each of us is the master of our own karma. This reality, rather than being the dogma of a religion, is the eternal nature of cosmic order.

Everything is dynamic, everything changes, and everything is in transit, including our emotions. So it's not uncommon to discover that after the fires of passion have cooled, those who had been so madly in love that they even defied parental objection now wonder what all that fuss was about.

To keep alive the wish to always be together two people should, rather than gazing at each other all the time, turn their eyes away from each other and turn them in the same direction. Rather than binding themselves to each other, they should give each other some room and make the effort to spend some time alone. The beautiful sounds of the zither come from strings that are separate yet parallel.

And that's the way it should be. *(1969)*

8. In Plenty of Time

No need to watch outsiders standing agape at the sight of Seoul's incredible development the last few years, for we can see it with our own eyes and feel it with our own hands. In contrast to the countryside, all of the investments are concentrated in Seoul—in politics, economics, education, and culture—to the point where we might as well call it "The Republic of Seoul" rather than its official name, "Seoul Special City." With the idea that even a beggar can make it in Seoul, the population continues to swell. But just because it is Seoul doesn't mean that everyone can enjoy the good life. In spite of the phenomenal modernization downtown, there are plenty of places within the city limits that haven't changed a bit.

If one were to talk about a ferryboat that goes back and forth across the river, a lot of people might imagine that you were talking about a provincial town. But it's not a provincial town. It's the ferry crossing at Ddukseom Islet in the big city of Seoul.

Along the riverside, there are hundreds of homes of good citizens who pay their taxes. But while the islet, too, is unquestionably part of Seoul Special City, it's still a sanctuary of the primitive—no electricity, no phones, and no running water. And the only transportation system is the ferryboat.

The ferryboat is really quite interesting. It is so unrelentingly of the people. And it is so nonjudgmental. It just gobbles up everyone and everything that comes its way. It takes on passenger cars and oxcarts and honey wagons, as well as men and women and children who stand on it rather indifferently. In addition, the ferry totally ignores the idea of a schedule. It moves only when it's full. It's useless for busy people to stomp their feet in frustration or indignation, because it's a boat without a sense of time, except between 10:00pm and 6:00am when it sleeps, and when it takes it easy during the rainy season flooding and when the river freezes over in winter.

People can never tell when the ferry is going to leave, so they often rush to the landing only to find that either the ferry has just left or that it's just sitting tied up on the other side waiting to fill up before coming back across.

So a few days ago I decided to change my thinking. Now whenever I have just missed the ferry, instead of grumbling and complaining, I think to myself, "I've got plenty of time till the next one." That way I can ease my mind rather than getting all uptight about having just missed it. Sure, maybe I lost some time, but why lose my wits as well?

When realizing how differently people respond to some of the same events in life, you can easily see how our reactions are emotional rather than rational. You might feel bad if you thought that something as beautiful as a rose had thorns. But then you could feel even grateful if you thought that something as worthless as a bunch of thorns could give blossom to something as beautiful as a rose. *(1969)*

9. Distant Sounds

Mornings are a feast of light green. Sunshine bouncing off the green leaves at the tips of the tree branches tempts me into opening the window, and as I do, fragrance from the dew-laden flowers floats into the room, taking my breath away. Orioles sing their tunes, magpies chat away, and pigeons coo to their mates. And I can hear the calls of the cuckoo faintly in the distance.

I hear the cuckoo every year at this time, and there is always something very quieting about the sound. It has a quality that is both maternal and eternal. It's a sound you never tire of, a sound that is always new.

Sometimes the distant call stops me in my tracks, no matter what I'm doing, and I stand against the wall to listen. Even though it's contrary to temple regulations to lean on anything, there's nothing cozier than leaning against the wall at such moments. The discriminating mind disappears and I become free of attachments, and then this emptied heart fills up with a feeling of gratitude for everything. In a sense, I almost feel like I have been conquered. Perhaps you wonder how the simple call of a bird could enrapture me this way but it is not just simply the call of the little cuckoo by itself. The call is brought by morning dew in May; by clear, bright sunlight; by the scent of flowers; by the intrinsic interrelationship of everything; and by things that even last night's stars didn't see. The little bird's call is the harmony of the entire universe.

When I listen to that distant call, I become freshly aware of a sense of oneness with everything that exists. At such moments I come to see that everything is flowing together like a timeless river, and I become thoroughly convinced of this reality. The invisible becomes clearer than the visible, and the eternal becomes closer than the present.

One of the tragedies of modernity is that artificial sounds are making it impossible to hear the sounds of eternity. They are cutting off the sounds that come from within the deepest part of us. *(1970)*

10. It's Raining

It's raining. The trees are getting soaked and the forest seems to be shimmering in the distance. The birds are searching for their nests. The subtle sound of the falling rain makes me drowsy enough to want to recline, to take it easy as if I had a lingering illness, to become kind and gentle.

People suddenly become more conscious of their own existence when they're ill, much more so than when they're feeling robust. In this silence I can, from deep inside, hear my inner voice and see my inner face. I envision my daily swaggering along the horizon, shadow and all. I wonder where that shadow came from and where it is headed. Like a recurring injury, that basic question once again rears its head: What's it all about?

We live in an age of noise. Noise awaits us as soon as we open our eyes and ears in the morning. We see all kinds of different noise in the morning editions of the newspapers. The ringing telephone is an announcement to us that we have no time to ourselves. We have to meet so-and-so at such and such a time, we give our opinions on all the world's affairs, and we sometimes even slander others as we gossip. In a world filled with media, the media are filled with people glaring at us and intimidating us with magic potions and the latest contraptions, telling us that we can't live without them. And having come to that state of affairs, we as people are no longer buried in noise—we have become the noisemakers. We are the noise itself.

People say that if they manage to escape noise even briefly, they become lonely and restless. That reflects how drugged we have become on noise. But being alone is in fact a chance for the routine self to return to the original self. Still, many can't stand being alone. And since we can't endure that quiet goodness at the base of our hearts, we have to gad about making more noise. So we flounder around in a self-created ruckus.

Words that are not based on quiet goodness, on purity and sincerity and gentleness, are in fact nothing but noise. The endless, meaningless talk that we pass back and forth all day long is no more than the noise of the marketplace. But the language that really moves our spirits, like majestic music, comes from the heart of silence and disappears back into it. Such silence, of course, carries with it the meaning and solemnity of words.

Having lost the true meaning of silence, of quiet goodness, people have become deaf to basic human questions. Instead, we continue to seek out new sounds, become entrapped by them, and wind up taking tonics and remedies to recover from the exhaustion that the new noise induces. Human relations built upon noise can only tire us out. Day by day this noise is detracting from our humanity.

The quest to rid ourselves of complete colonization by noise and to recover our sense of quiet goodness should be as necessary and perpetual as our quest to rid ourselves of air pollution.

It's raining.

Suddenly, I am swept up again with the desire to become kind and gentle, and to do something nice. The circus tent down by the river is probably getting soaked and has few visitors. When the weather clears, I'll meet a friend and we'll go to the circus. I'll be happy to pay double for two of the all-too-cheap entrance tickets to help them out, and enjoy everything that I missed the last time. *(1970)*

11. From the End of the Line

Our daily lives are filled with basically the same routines—some old gossip, a touch of interest here and there, and behavior based on a somewhat vague attitude toward life. Rather than constantly being mindful of our own behavior, we are content just to experience the ups and downs of our situations and to live rather banally.

Instead of depending on ourselves, we just flow along as if we've turned our lives over to inertia. It's easy for us to live within the limitations of imitation, formality, and habit, and to pass through life uneventfully. As a result, we gradually lose our own sense of liveliness and spontaneity.

That's all rather depressing; nevertheless we just go on without worrying about it. Still some people, in order to break out of this monotony, just take off and wander. Others may climb to the top of a bridge and cause a scene just to get into the news. But no matter what we do to escape our routines, they always seem to come back again like a shadow to haunt us.

Occasionally there are people strange enough to say that they wish that they could just start life all over. Once I suddenly took such a person out to a huge public cemetery at the end of the bus line. It's not that I was trying to be funny; rather, I wanted to show him something that would perhaps shed some new light on his dissatisfaction with life: death. The jam-packed graveyard was the perfect way.

If it weren't for the icy-looking tombstones standing over the graves, the place would probably seem quite serene. I wonder if all of those people are really lying there, having forgotten all their cares, and just soaking up the sound of the pine breezes overhead.

I wonder what all those countless people who have experienced death would like to say to us, the living.

And I wonder, if they were all called back from their deep, deep sleep, what they would do with their newfound lives.

They say that people on death row can really feel life every moment and every second because there is no tomorrow for them. They are intensely involved in the present. But although we are physically alive in the present, we always try to put life off until tomorrow. We don't regret carelessly wasting day after day even though each day is part of life.

People who really like Johaan Bach can probably feel things like the magnificence of a setting sun in his music because there is a certain depth to be found in the repetition. If there were no depth to be found through that repetition, then people would just pass off the music as simply another "nice tune."

People bored with their repetitive daily routines need to shed light on their lives from the end of the line, if for no other reason than to put some depth into the meaning of their existence. *(1970)*

12. The Early Matinee

Last Sunday on the way downtown I saw a long line in front of a theater and I couldn't help being impressed by the tenacity of the common people. But when I took a closer look at the faces of those standing silently under the blazing sun, thoughts of pity made me look again. I saw on their faces the shadow of exhaustion and gloom that you might find on the face of a wanderer far from home.

While others had probably taken advantage of the summer holiday to go to the shaded mountains or to the rolling sea to escape their monotonous routines, these people were glued like magnets to a zone of ceaseless pollution, and I couldn't help but feel a bit bad for them, even though their greatest fun was right in front of them—the theater.

Once in awhile I go to a movie myself but I've never been willing to stand in a long line in broad daylight. Since fun is directly tied to how you feel, the issue inevitably becomes related to time and place.

Awhile ago there was a local movie that was such an unusually big hit that the ads and critics led you to believe that you'd really regret not going to see it. I felt that way, too, so one day I went. Coming out of the theater after the movie, I had to stop in a drugstore to take something for the headache I got in the theater, but even that did little to soothe my misery. The movie itself wasn't all that bad but the theater was like a smelly, airtight storage room, and my head had begun to ache soon after the movie began. I had gone to the movies to enjoy myself and wound up suffering; yet the fault was mine for having let myself fall victim to the ads.

Ever since then I've preferred the early morning discount matinee. Not because of the discount but because of the atmosphere. First of all, you don't have to wait in line to get a ticket, so the formalities are simplified. You lose half the fun of going to the movies if you have to wait in a long line. Also, at the early matinee you have the special privilege of sitting anywhere you like. No need to try to follow the lead of the usherette with a dim flashlight, and there are empty seats all over the place. No need to strain your neck trying to see around the big head of someone in front of you. No nuisances like that at all.

But probably the greatest pleasure of all is the spaciousness. The purpose of going to a movie or play is to escape the monotony of our daily lives by entering into a new reality. But if the overcrowding in our daily lives spills over into the movie theater, too, then it's not worth going. We already have enough jam-packed commuter buses and in our neighborhoods, the eaves of the clustered houses just about touch one another. In a world that, in addition to being overcrowded, has also become hard-hearted, it is really nice to have the ease that comes with plenty of sitting room at the morning matinee.

When I sit in a theater like that with plenty of room, I am overtaken by waves of indescribable closeness with those scattered heads that I see in front of me. Funny that I feel close to those at a distance in an empty theater, and far from those sitting closest in a packed theater. I started wondering about who these people could be—people who couldn't find work? People who lost their jobs because they were too nice? Or people who just popped in on the way by?

I doubt that they would be the type of people who would ever give anyone a dirty look or who would pick a fight with someone for having stepped on their foot. Rather, they'd be the type of people who would be nice, gentle, and easy to communicate with.

On a summer morning last year, when I came out of a showing of *The 25th Hour* and saw traces of tears on a number of faces, I had the urge, out of joy, to suddenly shout, "You're the true poets and musicians!" and to grab their hands in friendship. *(1970)*

13. An Unforgettable Dharma Friend

Monk Suyon was both a Dharma friend and a genuine Dharma teacher to me. He never spoke of compassion—he just lived it. Just as sometimes an indifferent wildflower along a path can stop us in our tracks, he greatly moved me with his attention to even the smallest details.

He seldom spoke except to answer questions. Instead, he always kept a silent smile on his unforgettable face. I first met him fifteen years ago and still can't forget him.

In the fall of 1959, I readied myself for the upcoming three-month meditation season in an isolated hermitage near a major temple. The only things I had to prepare for the winter retreat were the food supply, firewood, and a bit of kimchi. Since my teacher Ven. Hyobong[1] had gone to Nepal for the World Buddhist Conference, I was left to do the retreat alone and my requirements were minimal.

In the tenth lunar month, about November, I went to a nearby farming area to collect offerings from the people. Over a period of five days I was able to collect enough supplies for the whole winter. When I made it back to the hermitage at twilight, I unexpectedly found smoke rising from the small kitchen chimney.

I put down my backpack and went to the kitchen, where an unfamiliar monk was stoking the fire. This wandering monk was dressed in quilted winter clothes and had a smile and a face as bright as the sun. With palms together he bowed to me. I bowed back. And that is how we met. It seems that people can make connections in a flash. This is even easier for people who have renounced the secular world and taken the vows of monkhood.

I was glad to hear that he had come for the winter meditation season. Although it may seem like total freedom to be able to do a meditation retreat alone, there are many more impediments than one might think when trying to make progress by oneself. Also, it hadn't been all that

[1] In 1923 he became Korea's first court judge but could not bear the role of sentencing others to death. He wandered for three years before taking the basic precepts, took full ordination and the Bodhisattva precepts in 1932, and received transmission in 1936.

long since I had taken the monastic vows, and frankly I was a bit afraid that I might become quite lazy in my practice if I did it alone.

Just before the full moon of the 10th lunar month, the day when the winter retreat begins each year, we sat down and decided on a number of things. He said that he would do whatever I asked him to do, but during a retreat there is no such thing as a host or a guest. The only way to get through a retreat is to compromise and work together. Yet Suyon didn't ask for a thing.

He was one year younger than me but had been a monk one year longer, so he was both junior and senior to me. I don't think he had much formal education yet he was very self-composed. Asking about such things as one's hometown and reasons for taking the vows is considered impolite among Buddhist monks, so Suyon and I had no idea about each other's backgrounds. Those things are irrelevant to monks anyway. The present is imminently important.

We decided that I would cook the rice and he would take care of the soup and side dishes. And he wasn't just your average cook. He could bring the best flavor out of even the worst ingredients. We also agreed that I would clean the Buddha Hall and the toilet while he would clean the meditation hall and the kitchen.

We decided to have just one meal a day and to pour all of our efforts into meditation. We observed the precepts with the fervor of newly ordained monks and totally ignored the outside world in order to make as much progress as possible.

We were nearing completion of that winter retreat and it had gone well without any hitches. That in itself is rather unusual. In retrospect it is not easy to complete an entire three-month session without something going wrong somewhere or people getting on each other's nerves.

The winter retreat finishes on the full moon of the first lunar month, usually in February. As the end of the retreat approached, we talked about nothing but traveling around together and visiting other temples during the free three-month period between retreats.

But on the day before the end of the retreat, I started to get sick. I thought perhaps it might have been due to an ice-cold bath I had taken a few days earlier. Regardless, in gaining a fever I had lost my appetite. And I started to get the chills. Even though the retreat was over, I was in no condition to go anywhere.

There's nothing worse than getting sick up in the mountains. Of course, a monk's life is a lonely one but you really feel it even more when you're sick. There's no medicine and there are no medical facilities around. All you can do is just let the illness run its course. At such times, monks really realize how totally possessionless we are in this life. But when I moaned in the night, Suyon would be right there to sit with me. He brought me water when I thirsted and he stayed up throughout the night to put cold towels on my feverish head.

One morning he said that he was going down to the village below and that he would be right back. But there was no sign of him by noon, or even as the sun sank into the horizon. I had some leftover porridge for supper, and then I began to worry.

I must have dozed off for awhile but around ten o'clock at night I heard someone in the kitchen. Suddenly Suyon opened the door and came into the room with a bowl of warm, fragrant oriental herb medicine. He apologized for being so late and told me to drink the concoction. It's something I'll never forget. His kindness moved me to tears. Without a word, he just grabbed onto my hand and held it.

The nearest herbalist to the hermitage was at least twenty kilometers away. The only real transportation in those days were the trucks that shuttled people back and forth from villages every market day, but that day had not been a market day. So Suyon must have hiked a total of more than forty kilometers to the herbalist and back.

Since neither of us had a penny, he must have gone all the way to the town, gone chanting door-to-door to collect money for the medicine, and then bought the remedy at the shop. Then he came all the way back in the dark and boiled the herbs in the kitchen.

That was the first time in my life that I could really feel, with body and soul, the nature of unfettered compassion. I really experienced the genuine warmth that is part of having a true Dharma friend. Is there any disease in the world that couldn't be overcome just with that kind of sincerity and kindness? The next day I was up and about, albeit my legs were a bit wobbly.

About three kilometers from our hermitage, up in the thick forest, an old meditating monk lived in a makeshift hut beside a waterfall. Whenever he had to go down the mountain for something, he always dropped by to see us on his way back. However, on the way back up his brimming backpack always got to our hermitage before he did. Suyon, sensing when he would return, would go down to meet him and then carry the backpack up the mountain for him each and every time. Whenever there was something to be done, Suyon always did it as quickly and as quietly as possible.

The retreat was over, and although we had previously mused on traveling around together during the free season, we had our separate ways to go, so we didn't see each other for a long time. And there was no way to keep track of each other either during the wandering season, so I suppose that we just felt that no news must be good news.

Some might think of that as a pretty cold way to treat each other after spending three months together, but actually it is in deep consideration of trying not to interfere with each other's progress. There's an old saying in the Sangha that too much natural affection is an impediment on the Path. Attachments deny us the freedom that we are searching for. Our quest is liberation, which is the overcoming of all restraints and reaching that state of total freedom. Restraints don't just come out of nowhere—they are born out of attachments. And human attachments are much stronger than material attachments. The real meaning of renunciation, or "leaving home" when entering the monkhood, is renouncing the world of attachment. So in one sense, the more cold-hearted a new monk is, the greater his resolve is likely to be in striving for enlightenment.

Such apparent indifference is a negative on the way to becoming a positive. It is part of the process of sublimating natural personal affection into compassion for all forms of life. The warmth of a bodhisattva standing on the horizon of compassion is like the warmth of the gentle spring sun.

For the summer meditation retreat I went to "Snowbound Hall" (perhaps I thought just the name might keep me cool for the summer) at Haeinsa Temple and I heard that Suyon was in a prayer session at a temple quite far away. So I thought that after my retreat I would go visit him. But he came to see me first. We hadn't seen each other since we had meditated together so we were quite happy to meet again. He still had that silent smile on his face, but he didn't look as healthy as he had when we had meditated together. I asked him what was wrong and he said he had digestive problems. I suggested that he take something for it but he said that he was OK.

He stayed at Snowbound Hall and immediately there were noticeable changes around the place. There was something different about the step in front of the hall. Every day the dozen or so pairs of white monks' shoes were as clean as fresh snow and lined up in perfect order. Suyeon and his silent work again. And when the elder monks took off their robes to launder, the robes would be washed, starched, and ironed before anyone knew it. The monks started to refer to Suyon as "Bodhisattva of Compassion."

At Snowbound Hall, since we were with other monks in a large group, we were eating three regular meals a day rather than one as Suyon and I had done before. But Suyon didn't each much at all. So one day I reported to the temple office and then dragged a very unwilling Suyon off to a doctor in the nearest town. He was having real digestive problems and I felt that he needed an examination and, if necessary, medical treatment.

While we were in the bus on the way, Suyon took out a small knife from his pocket and screwed in two loose screws on the window frame. This startled me but I tried to look unmoved. He had the ability to unsettle me with something as insignificant as this. He never seemed to discriminate between "mine" and "yours." Who knows, maybe he just thought that everything was his as a result of realizing that nothing was his. He was really somebody who could own the whole world.

We spent the next winter meditation at Haeinsa as well. The monks who were worried about his health told him to take a separate room so that he could have freedom of movement if he needed it. But he declined and sat in meditation with the rest of us and did everything a monk was expected to do during the retreat.

But about halfway through the retreat he could no longer hold up. The temple was no place for treatment, so I took him to stay at a propagation hall in a nearby city so that he could receive whatever treatment was necessary. But Suyon was more concerned about my break from meditation than about himself. After three days there, he told me to return to the meditation session at Haeinsa. He looked much better so I agree and asked the monk in charge of the propagation hall to look after him for a while. I returned to the temple a couple of days later even though I felt bad about leaving him. I heard from time to time afterwards that he was recovering.

It snowed a lot that winter at Haeinsa. In fact the snow got so deep that the roads were blocked and there was no transportation for about a week. At night the valleys echoed with the sound of branches snapping in the snow. While out collecting fallen branches for firewood, I happened to sprain my right ankle and it took awhile to get over it, even with regular acupuncture treatment. During that time I received a small package in the mail. I opened it only to find that it was filled with an ointment for sprains. Suyon, who was at another temple quite far away, had sent it, although I had no idea how he knew about my condition. Silent Suyon never missed a thing.

I don't want to ruminate on Suyon's sad demise. But after he was gone, I came to realize that he had clearly been my alter ego. We hadn't been together even a full year but he taught me so very much during that time. To me he was a real Dharma friend and a shining Dharma teacher, even more so than a Zen or Sutra teacher, because he taught the best way possible—through example.

On the path to seeking truth, what we know is so trifling compared to how we behave. Suyon brought me to the realization of how much we affect one another, but not through our knowledge or speech. He was a perfect model of how spirits can communicate through a clear look, a quiet smile, the warmth of a kind hand, silent behavior.

Like a brilliant lotus growing out of murky water, Suyon always silently brightened everything around him. He exemplified the path of equanimity. I never even once saw him get angry. In a word, he was the incarnation of composure and compassion.

Every time I think of him, I'm reminded again that it's not how long we live but how we live that's so important. *(1970)*

14. Nothing Ever Existed

Practically from the moment we are born we start building karma with things, many of which we couldn't possibly live without. The old saying that man is lord of all creation exemplifies the interdependent relationship that we have with things.

When people achieve harmony between what they want and what they have, then they tend to kick back and relax. Yet at the same time, some things that people want can actually cause a lot of grief and anger. And of this grief and anger, what is most upsetting comes from the concept of ownership.

Look at the grief people suffer when they lose something that they valued highly. Such an occasion teaches us how deeply ingrained our attachments are. We can even say that in a sense it's a double loss, since you often lose both the object and your senses. In such a case, it's best for your own mental health to get over the attachment and have a change of heart.

We were born with nothing, and if you really look closely, there's nothing that you can really call your own. Things come to us through karma and when the karma is over they leave us. In other words, since I don't exist separately, how can I own something that also doesn't exist separately? Things are with us for a while, and that's all. Bundles of transiting karma come to visit with us, we who are also bundles of transiting karma, and then leave, just like we sometimes leave them.

On occasion temples in the countryside that don't have walls get robbed. One night a thief snuck into a hermitage out in the middle of nowhere. An old monk who didn't sleep well went to the outhouse and on his return he heard something in the backyard. Someone was there with an A-frame that was loaded up, but the robber couldn't lift up his loaded A-frame no matter how many times he tried. He had put a sack of rice from the storage bin on the A-frame and it proved to be too heavy to lift.

The old monk snuck up behind the A-frame and the next time the thief tried to lift it the monk gave it a push. As soon as the robber lifted it up, he glanced around behind him.

The monk simply whispered, "Don't say a word. Just go." The old monk must have figured that anyone who would steal rice from a temple must have really needed it.

The next morning the other monks were in an uproar over the fact that a thief had come during the night and stolen the rice. But the old monk didn't say anything at all, because he hadn't lost anything.

Nothing ever existed. This term is used on a different level in the world of Zen, but it is also used concerning the concept of ownership. Nothing is ever ours.

Rumor had it that not long after the incident, the thief became one of the most devout lay people at the hermitage. *(1970)*

15. Maternal Love in the Sutras

The Buddha Sakyamuni lost his own mother when he was only a week old and was raised by his maternal aunt Mahapajapati. So the Bodhisattva never really knew his mother's face or voice, her gentle eyes, her warmth. Of course his aunt raised him like her own son, but still he had had a precious gift taken from him.

Later, after he had become enlightened and began to teach, he occasionally talked about a mother's love. And whenever he talked about compassion, he always described it as "the love a mother has for her child."

When we truly love someone, where is there a standard to measure such love? Some say that love is giving, but true love is being able to willingly give even your life for that love. And a mother can do that readily and unhesitatingly for her child. That is true compassion and true love.

In love between the sexes and love in other interpersonal relationships, it is easy to think in terms of what you are getting out of the relationship one way or another. But a mother's love is clear and absolute, and it is unconditional. It is not based on some philosophy or thought system. Rather it is an intrinsic part of life itself.

There are innumerable Buddhist sutras that expound upon the love a mother has for her child. Often the moral of these sutras is that filial piety is a natural way to repay the benevolence bestowed upon us through parental love.

Also, it is of interest to note that in the early sutras the mother always came first, as in "mother and father." This expression was used in some of the earlier Upanishads but it became practically universal in the sutras. One sutra states that our greatest benefactors are, in order, "mother, father, the Buddha, and a preaching monk." When Buddhism began to spread throughout a Confucian, patriarchal China, however, "mother and father" became "father and mother" in the Chinese translations.

Interestingly enough, we also find in the sutras that in ancient India names were taken from the mother's family. Sariputta was one of the Buddha's disciples, and his name meant "son of Sari," with Sari being his mother's name. There are many instances of such naming.

Perhaps the most famous sutra in Korea dealing with maternal love is the Parental Benevolence Sutra, which is thought to be Chinese in origin. In Korea the oldest copy dates to 1553CE and the Sutra is often depicted in woodprints hundreds of years old and more recently in paintings as well. An abbreviated version of the sutra follows:

> One day as the Buddha was traveling south with his followers, he came across a pile of bones on the path and he immediately prostrated before them with great reverence. His disciple Ananda asked him how such a revered person as the Buddha could prostrate himself before a pile of bones.
>
> The Buddha replied, "Ananda, I am bowing because these bones could be those of parents from a previous existence. Take a careful look. Male bones are white and heavy, but female bones are dark and lightweight. Female bones are dark and heavy because women lose a tremendous amount of blood with each birth, as well as immeasurable milk in breast-feeding each child. The suffering to their systems results in dark, lightweight bones."

The Buddha then went on to explain the ten parental benevolences.

"The first benevolence is that of prenatal care, when the mother's concerns all shift to the newly conceived child. The second benevolence is the pain of childbirth. The mother is filled with dread and her bones feel like they are being torn apart during childbirth, but she endures for her child's sake. The third is forgetting her own fears and replacing them with worry and concern for the newborn child.

The fourth benevolence is swallowing the bitter so that the child may taste the sweet. If necessary, a mother would starve herself to make sure that her child is fed. The fifth benevolence is that a mother will sleep on a wet spot to insure that the baby is dry, and she often goes without sleep worrying over the child.

Next is feeding and rearing. The mother is indifferent to her own afflictions and is preoccupied with her child's well being. The seventh benevolence is keeping the child clean day and night. The eighth benevolence is worrying about an absent child. When a child leaves home, a mother's heart follows both day and night as she waits for the child's return.

The ninth benevolence is worrying about a child's welfare and taking on her child's pain. The child's hardships become her own. Finally, the tenth and last benevolence is eternal love and concern. A child may grow up and leave its mother, but a mother never forgets her child. A 100-year-old mother still worries about her 80-year-old child."

The Buddha continued: "Having done all of this, a mother hopes that her child will attain maturity, but some children grow up unaware of all of this benevolence and may even maltreat their mother. They may answer a mother with insolence and even curse her. They may ignore the father, even if he is naked and hungry, and care only about dressing and feeding themselves. Parental virtue is endless, but it's impossible to fully describe the ingratitude of children."

> The Buddha's followers began to regret all of their own misdeeds and asked repeatedly how they could repay such parental benevolence.
>
> The Buddha answered, "If a grown child bore his father on one shoulder and his mother on the other and carried them around Mt. Sumeru until his skin wore to the bone and the bone wore to marrow; if a child carried his parents this way around Mt. Sumeru 100,000 times, he could still not repay the karmic indebtedness to his parents."

It is easy for practicing monks to forget the benevolence of their parents, and that is one reason why such sutras as this were composed. The Buddha emphasized that the monks should go beyond blood lines and in fact respect all sentient beings as they would respect their parents and treat all as members of a universal family.

The Story of Hariti

We are unfamiliar with many Buddhist sutras, and the reason why some are not so well known is that at first the stories do not seem to relate directly to Buddhist teachings. However, once you delve into them, the Buddhist meaning becomes clear. And often the folktales from long ago that we were told as children in Korea have hints of basic Buddhism in them.

Ethnic Korean thought emerged as a distinct entity from the mixing of innumerable stories and fables. Indian thought, and for that matter any ethnic thought, is no exception to this rule. Naturally in the process of its development, Buddhism carried and transmitted innumerable narratives and a wealth of literature from its pre-Buddhist Indian heritage, and much of this cultural background can be found in the teachings. The following is another abbreviated version of a sutra story:

> Once upon a time, there lived a *raksha* (ghost) on a mountain outside the Magada capital of Rajagraha, and he was revered for protecting the land. He sent his daughter off to marry Pancika, the son of another *raksa* in Gandara. One day when

the couple was out strolling in the mountains, the woman said that she wanted to go back home to Rajagraha to gobble up all the children. Pancika protested, saying that she could never do that to the children in her own hometown.

The couple eventually had 500 children of their own and as soon as the children had grown some, the wife ghost started to get weird ideas again. The husband scolded her again, but this time to no avail. One day she snuck out of the house and returned to Rajagraha, where she stole children out of their mothers' arms and gobbled them up. Every day the city lived in fear. So the people went and appealed to the king to have the ghost captured so that she could no longer steal their children. After numerous appeals, the king forbade anyone to leave the city, but that didn't work. A fortuneteller even held an offering service for the raksha god, but that failed, too. The terror within the city continued to grow, and the ghost who devoured the children came to be known as Hariti raksa, the mother of little ghosts.

The Buddha heard this story. The next morning he went into the city to collect meal offerings like he did everyday and after returning to the temple, he went to Hariti's home nearby, but she had gone out again to gobble up more children. Although she was out some of her children were playing in the house, so the Buddha took her dearly beloved youngest son back to the temple with him. When Hariti returned home, she nearly lost her mind. She spent the next couple of days running around the streets screaming out for her child.

Finally, she appeared before the Buddha and pleaded with him. "Oh Buddha, someone has stolen my youngest and I think I'm going to go mad. Please, out of your compassion, find him and rescue him for me!"

The Buddha said, "I'm so sorry that you lost your darling youngest. How many children did you have?"

"Altogether, five hundred."

"Five hundred! That's quite a number. So missing one shouldn't be such a big deal."

> "Not so," she replied. "It doesn't matter how many children you have—each one is precious. If I can't find this child, I'll cough up blood and die!"
>
> "If you are having such a fit over losing just one of so many, how could you steal children from women who had only one or two of their own? Think of the sorrow of a woman who has lost her only son. Your loss can't even begin to be compared to the loss of others."
>
> This brought Hariti to her senses. "I now realize what I have done. I won't do it again."
>
> After the Buddha got her to promise to behave, he returned her youngest son to her. The city returned to normal. Hariti repented her sins and took refuge in the Triple Gem of the Buddha, the Dharma and the Sangha. And she then became the Guardian Goddess of Childbirth and Children.

The story teaches not just about a perverted sense of motherhood, but also the Buddhist moral that one should love all children as one's own. *(1971)*

16. Possessionless

We are born empty-handed and when the time comes to go, we leave empty-handed, so it's no accident that Korean burial clothes don't have a single pocket. But in between birth and death, we come into our own share of things. Of course, a lot of these are things we use in daily life; but of those, how many of them are absolutely essential?

There are lots of things that we really do need but sometimes possessions can also be a burden. How much we possess can actually determine how confined we are. If possessions begin to tie us down, they begin to possess us rather than the other way around. Nowadays it's fashionable to brag about quantities, but that, too, carries with it the implication that the more one has, the more confined he is.

Three years ago a friend gave me two orchids and I treated them with as much attention and tender loving care as possible. I got books and read up on orchids. I went out and bought plant food for them. I was careful to put them in a shady spot during the hot summer; and in the winter I had to keep the temperature low indoors to guarantee an inactive period. If I had devoted that much attention to my parents when I was young, I probably would have been praised as a really good son.

This past spring the orchids rewarded me for all that attention by presenting me with light green flowers and subtle, totally captivating fragrances. Everyone who came to visit loved the freshly blossomed orchids with their scintillating scent.

Then this summer, on one of the rare sunny days during the monsoon season, I went to visit a senior monk at another temple. I was walking up the path toward the temple around midday. The brilliant sunshine fell as steadily as the rains had fallen during the monsoons, and the cicadas sang their hearts out, making a perfect accompaniment to the lively sound of the flowing stream.

As I soaked up that scene, I suddenly remembered that I had left the orchids out in the front yard at my place. The bright sunshine that I had been celebrating suddenly became an enemy as I envisioned the orchids wilting away. So I turned around and hurried back. And sure enough, the leaves had already wilted. I fetched some springwater and that finally revived them to a degree; but even after they came around, they weren't quite as fresh and lively as before.

That's when I really felt that attachment could be a source of pain. I had been too fixated on the orchids. So I made up my mind right there and then to break that attachment. The orchids had immobilized me to the point where I had to stay put and couldn't even travel about like the other monks during the free seasons between meditation retreats. Also, if I went out at all, it was always only briefly, and if the orchids were inside, I left the door slightly ajar so that they'd have a little change of air. On other occasions, I had gone out only to hurry back, having suddenly realized that I had left the plants outside. That was indicative of a really strong fixation. I could hardly make a move without considering the orchids.

So a few days later, I gave the orchids to a visiting friend who was as quiet as an orchid himself. I had liberated myself from the confinement and I felt as free as a bird in the sky. Even though I had sent off those three-year-long friends, I felt more lighthearted than empty-hearted.

It was from then on that I made up my mind to get rid of one thing a day. The orchids had taught me the real meaning of being possessionless.

In one sense you could even interpret the history of humanity as a desire to possess. History is filled with battles for more and more. The desire to possess has no limits and it never even takes a single day off, and desire is not just for things—it's for other people as well. Look at the endless human tragedies that result when one person doesn't get someone they really want. We can't even control our own minds, and yet out of the desire to possess more, we try to control others.

This desire to possess decreases proportionately with an increase in understanding the nature of that desire, not only on the personal level but on the national level as well. We can easily see that both at home and abroad some of yesterday's allies have become enemies, while some of yesterday's enemies are becoming friends—all based on self-interest in the quest for more of something. It makes you wonder what the history of the world might be like if we eliminated the quest to possess. There probably wouldn't be any more confrontations. People and nations wouldn't be fighting over what they didn't get.

Mahatma Gandhi once said that to him the act of possession was like a form of crime. He said that he wouldn't possess something unless everyone else who wanted it had it as well. Since that would be impossible, he felt that his possessing anything would carry as much guilt as a sin or a crime.

We are sometimes blinded by this desire to possess to the point where we even forget who we are. Nevertheless, one day each one of us will have to leave empty-handed. We'll not only leave behind our bodies; there's not a thing we can do about our possessions once we're gone.

People who rid themselves of much gain much. To use a common adage, less is more. People confined or hurt by things should really think about this: Being possessionless also means that when you don't claim a single thing as your own, the whole world is yours. *(1971)*

17. On the Road

People have all kinds of hobbies that provide fun, inspiration, and flexibility. And any hobby has the potential to build character.

I can't imagine anyone not liking travel. Some people are confined to the home, but for most of us just the mention of travel is enough to make our hearts flutter. We may not have the financial leeway or the time, but who could ever deny the lightheartedness and endless excitement of being on the road?

Nothing is more fun than breaking out of our suffocating routines. And when we hit the road in the spring, we find ourselves whistling just like the starlings. Once you just pack up and head out, you can really get at least a vague feeling for what life is all about. You take your shadow with you and you can take a good look at how far you have come as you plod along toward that vague horizon. You can come to understand why Herman Hesse loved the clouds and why Antoine de Saint-Exupery extolled the stars. While wandering in a strange area, sometimes you can even be brushed by a delicate, even tasty sense of melancholy.

Last fall I wandered about the country for nearly a month. But a monk's wanderings are not quite the same as those of secular people. Monks have no destination in mind and no one is waiting for them. They just follow their hearts and their feet. It's called "floating like the clouds and flowing like the waters."

It has long been the Buddhist tradition to alternately meditate for three months and then wander for three months. But the three months of wandering aren't meant to be for sightseeing. The period is an opportunity for monks to spread Buddhism as they go, to seek out other teachers, and to make more progress on the Buddhist path amid the ways of the secular world.

Of course, while wandering I spend my nights in temples, usually unfamiliar ones. Hearing the evening bell at sunset at the wooded entrance to a temple; cooling off my feet and washing off the sweat in the cold temple stream; and enjoying the fragrance from a cup of tea while catching up on all the latest from other monks—such things sweep away the weariness that results from travel.

I spent last fall this way—like the clouds, just following my feet as they went north, south, east, and west. So I had the chance to ruminate on my life since taking ordination. And each time I thought about my life as a monk, memories passed over me like breezes from a stream. Sometimes I felt happy; sometimes I felt embarrassed.

But while wandering, there was one place I would not go. Actually I was afraid to go there because I wanted to. It was a place I always wanted to save as special, the place where I had stayed a short time after I had first taken ordination. It was the place where I learned the real meaning of practice, a place where I found the joy of Zen meditation through intensive practice.

About sixteen years ago, my teacher Ven. Hyobong and I spent a three-month retreat together in a mountain hermitage. The only written material that I had ever received from my master was a copy of *Compilation of Caution for the Initiate*. Yet during that retreat with my teacher, daily life itself was enough to heavily influence me.

I was in charge of cooking the rice and preparing the side dishes. Of course I meditated a lot. But when we ran out of supplies, I would go out to collect offerings in the villages and if we needed something else, I'd have to go to the nearest town with a market, about twenty kilometers away.

One day when I went to the market I happened to buy a novel. After bedtime at 9 p.m., I went into the rest area of the hermitage, lit a small kerosene lamp, and started reading. Since it was the first non-Buddhist scripture that I had read since taking ordination, I was really soaking it up when the door suddenly opened. It was my teacher. As soon as he saw the book he told me to take it out and burn it. He said that to read such a book was a violation of my vows of renunciation and that true renunciation meant leaving everything secular behind.

So I went out and burned the book, the first time I had ever done such a thing. At first I felt bad about it and thought it was a waste, but after a few days I came to realize the limitation of books. A book is only one type of vehicle for transmitting information and that all one really gets out of books is just a greater sense of fractionalization and classification. In order to deepen the wisdom of nondiscrimination, one has to carefully filter concentration.

Up until that time, I had often thought about the books that I had left behind at home when I had become a monk, but by burning that single book, I also burned away all those concerns. I had come to realize that in those early days as a monk, the discriminations that books had promoted in my mind served only as barriers to progress on the Path. Had I not burned that book, perhaps I would have continued to live weighed down by books.

And something else happened during that retreat. We had run out of side dishes so I went down to the nearest village to replenish our supply. I was about ten minutes late getting back to prepare lunch. My master said, "Let's fast today, if your concept of time is that bad."

During the retreat, we had been having porridge for breakfast, rice with side dishes for lunch, and nothing after that. So the reprimand for my carelessness in letting an elder monk go hungry was something that I reflected upon time and time again during the retreat. I learned a lot from that reprimand. It was hard to find a place of practice that afforded such lessons in character building, since many of the temples were becoming either tourist attractions or quiet cramming quarters for high school students before college entrance exams.

When you're wandering on the road, you can feel the weight of your spirit. It's a chance to take a good look at your real self and to see what and how you're doing. So traveling is much more than just a kind of hobby or interest. It's an opportunity to seriously put yourself back in order and to find new meaning in life.

And it's a great way to practice for when you're getting ready to leave this world. *(1971)*

18. Written Wills

When the time comes to die, we should just die quietly instead of making a fuss about the whole thing. And although some people preparing to commit suicide may feel the need to leave a note to rationalize the act, such written excuses are hardly warranted for people who have lived as long as they should. Besides, words, whether written or spoken, are invariably accompanied by misunderstandings.

In addition, we never know when death will sneak up on us. There are so many ways to go unexpectedly—traffic accidents, gas poisoning from the charcoal briquette heating system, or an unknown someone from a former life stalking us to seek revenge. When we consider the fact that, from the point of view of death, what we consider to be living is actually dying one step at a time, we can see that living is dying and dying is living, and life and death are inexorably intertwined, inseparable. We should always be ready to stand up and answer whenever and wherever death calls out our name.

So rather than leaving a written will, I'd rather live a life that's an open book. Besides, we only live once and since I am a monk, there's nothing about me that demands a will. The only reason why I'm writing this in the first place is that a newspaper editor asked me to do so for an article. So I'm doing it in a lighthearted way.

And besides, for whom would I write a will?

There's no one, since I am completely alone. Even the Buddha in whom I take refuge is an outsider to me. I came into this world alone and I'll have to leave alone. I've just been dragging my shadow along the horizon of life and I'll continue to do so until it's time to go. So there's no one for me to write a will for.

Of course, my life has been possible over the years through cooperative efforts of lots of people, both close and distant. And of course I'll continue to live that way. But since the nature of existence as we know it is an individual one, when it comes down to it, each one of us is all alone. I'm not romanticizing here. I'm just stating an undeniable basic fact about the nature of existence.

Ludwig van Beethoven, who broke through the world of torment into the world of joy, had something to say about all of this. The only thing he felt that humanity held over the rest of the animal kingdom was a basic goodness. He felt that even though the earth was darkened by contradictions, conflicts, hate, war, and killings, it was humanity's basically good nature that made the sun rise in the morning.

So before leaving this world, the first thing that I have to do is repent for having trashed this basic goodness. If I don't repent for such foolish misdeeds as taking advantage of the good nature of others, I won't be able to die in peace.

There are times when small misdeeds bother us more than the larger ones. The greater misdeeds can weigh on us so heavily that the shame involved can blind us to them, and so we tend to remember the smaller ones. This in itself can be a major form of hypocrisy. Regardless, over my lifetime there was one small thing that still fills me with a sense of irrevocable regret and guilt. It's like a shadow that follows me around, both embarrassing and bothering me from time to time in flashbacks.

It was in middle school. On our way home after school, a handful of classmates and I came upon a taffy vendor who was taking a break. I had seen him before from time to time in front of the school gate, and had noticed that he had a bad arm and that he stuttered. Anyway, we gathered around him pretending to pick the best pieces of taffy and in the process snitched quite a few while paying for only a couple of pieces. The handicapped vendor, of course, didn't know the difference.

I can't undo this thing from the past, and it still bothers me. If he were a smart, healthy taffy vendor, I would have already forgotten about the whole incident. But the fact that he was handicapped compounds my sense of guilt.

During my life I've done more than my share of misdeeds and I can't even count the unforgivable ones. But for some reason, the snitching incident haunts me like a ghost. I have to repent for this and I fervently hope that in my next life I'll not repeat such a thing. I've gotten by so far in life by considering such things as betrayals and incriminations as payback for what I had done to the handicapped taffy vendor.

I can fully understand a quote from the Upanishads that the path to becoming a sage is as hard as walking on a road of blades.

Since there's nothing I can take with me when I leave this earth, there's no need for me to hassle others with a will. Monks live with the philosophy that "nothing ever existed." But just in case there are any books that I liked or any books for which I had written a forward, I'd like to pass them on to the kid who brings the newspaper every morning and evening.

Funerals and memorial services are useless; yet nowadays some monks have funerals that even outdo some secular ones. Such a funeral for me, rather than being a source of consolation, would do nothing but anger me, since, like my meals, I like things that are "simple and plain." And if I were to have a grave, I'd rather have some of those summer poppies or sunflowers planted on it than have a frigid looking gravestone. But since I won't have a grave, I won't be putting anyone to that added trouble.

A corpse is a dreadful thing to look at once the life force is gone and it becomes a burden to the living. So I'd be grateful to have it disposed of as quickly as possible. It would be nothing more than an old set of clothes. A cremation anywhere would be fine so long as it did not prove to be a burden to anyone. And I certainly hope there would be no remaining relics that would become a nuisance for others.

After leaving the body, there's one place where I would really love to fly away to, and that is the Little Prince's star, a star so tiny that just by moving my chair a bit, I could see a number of spectacular sunsets each day. Right now I wonder if the Little Prince, who knew that looking in to your own heart was the most important thing, is having fun with the roses. I'd really like to go there to visit that planet, since there aren't even any bothersome immigration procedures.

And in my next life, I'd really like to be reborn on the Korean Peninsula. Regardless of what others may say about a monk's life of nonattachment, my love for the language is so great that I hate to give it up. And I want to return as a monk again to finish up what I won't be able to achieve in this life. *(1971)*

19. Lotus in the Murky Waters

I heard from a friend that the lotuses had blossomed in a pond at one of the royal palaces in Seoul, so the next day I hurried there to see them. It was fantastic. The pond was filled with spotless green lotus pads and pink lotus blossoms had risen, majestically and immaculately, above them. Breezes wafting across the pond filled me with wave after wave of the subtle fragrances. I just walked around and around in a seemingly mutual osmosis of lotus and spirit until sunset.

A lotus can't blossom on a mountaintop or on dry land; it blossoms only out of murky waters and when it does blossom it seems to make the murkiness disappear. One forgets entirely about the concept of filth. I think that's because, thanks to the perfection of the lotus, everything around it seems to become as clear and bright as the flower itself. In addition, on its journey up through the muddy waters, the lotus doesn't permit a single drop of murky water to stick to it. The nature of the lotus is to remain pure and spotless even while living amidst the dark and dirty.

People can't live alone. From the time we are born we are destined to interact and live with innumerable others. Once we're grown, we manage our lives in complicated and delicate relationships. But those relationships aren't always as clear and fragrant and as beautiful as the lotus. Problems arise when those relationships become as messy and stinky and dirty as the lotus pond. Our lives are filled with contradictions and conflicts and absurdities, and there are plenty of times when they're noisy and messy. But that is our reality, whether we like it or not.

Our lives are our own lotus ponds. They belong to no one else. Thus we cannot get along just by following and imitating others. We have to make our own lives. And in order to do so, it is essential first to establish our own convictions.

The way of the lotus is to grow spotlessly out of murky waters in order to brighten everything around it. I find this a great inspiration to making progress on the Path. *(1972)*

20. Soil and Space

A popular adage nowadays in the countryside is, "You can live without a wife but you can't live without your galoshes!" In our section of Seoul, the adage applies all the way down to the ferry landing on the river. The mud is from a new roadway development project.

Up until even a couple of years ago, the road went around the sides of the hills, and with rice paddies and banks of vegetable plots, the area had a completely rustic atmosphere. It was countryside in the city. But for the sake of some district development, the city leveled the hills, filled in the rice paddies, and flattened all of the fields. The area became nothing but a stretch of level land. There were no drainage ditches so when it rained or when snow melted, the place became a mess. Yet the people didn't complain a bit to the authorities and, as gentle as lambs, they just continued coming and going as usual.

Now that the winter ice has melted, it's hard walking around here even with your galoshes on. Yet I continue to trudge along with a sense of gratitude, since I have rediscovered what I had been missing for some time.

Several of us had a temple project to complete, so we all moved into a new apartment complex in this area for about a month. Everyone felt that it would be too inconvenient to stay in a temple for that length of time to complete the project at hand. At first, we all adapted pretty well to the change of environment. Perhaps it was the newness of it all. We developed an inquisitiveness about everything around us and had the new opportunity to experience apartment-style living. This arrangement was quite convenient and thus saved us time in some ways. But as the days passed, our productivity failed to increase, and we even felt as if we were falling behind schedule.

From the eighth floor of the apartment building, all we had to do was press an elevator button and we were soon back on the ground. From there, it was only about twenty steps to a supermarket, so we could easily buy whatever we needed. If even that was too much of a bother, all we had to do was call, place an order and wait for delivery. And with central heating, we didn't have to worry about collecting wood or lighting charcoal briquettes for heat. Yet even though we had all these conveniences, things weren't going so smoothly. There was something missing and I couldn't figure out what it was.

One day while trudging through the mud in my galoshes, it hit me: Living comfortably didn't necessarily mean living well. Since moving to the apartment, we had stopped walking. There's a lot more to walking than just exercise. It's invigorating. And it makes you think more clearly. But by living in an apartment building and taking the elevator, we had stopped walking.

In addition, our vision had become restricted due to the adjacent apartment blocks. An open vista promotes a feeling of infinity. But with all the apartments around, the area where we were staying had become vertical. It lacked horizontal space. We were also cut off from our neighbors and the people in the same elevator were complete strangers. Worst of all, there was no soil. So that was the source of the problem: Since there was no scent of the soil—humanity's eternally friendly fragrance—we had been living in an abstract world, a controlled environment.

How can people expect to thrive by turning their backs on soil and open space? Yet modern people seem to be searching only for comfort. In this overriding quest for comfort, they are forgetting about soil and space. Of course, there is something healthy in the process of overcoming inconveniences—even the inconveniences of flatlands and distance and mud; but we are now losing the sense of finding value even in the very process of overcoming difficulties.

Although I can live with inconveniences and galoshes, I can't live very long without soil and space. *(1972)*

21. Tick Tock, A Karmic Clock

Meeting someone new can often be awkward; but, on the other hand, sometimes you can actually wind up feeling grateful.

There are 3.6 billion people living in the world and out of all of those, I met one today. And I can't help but be grateful for that karma. Particularly when in Korea—even though we all live under the same sky, speak the same language, and share the same custom—we usually just pass one another by.

But even if we were to meet a potential enemy, could that meeting be anything but karma? Of all the people around, why is it that this person and I ran into each other? According to the laws of karma, the time was ripe.

And it seems that there's karma with objects as well as with people. Of all the objects in the world, a certain clock came to me. Right in front of me, as I write on this desk, this clock of unknown nationality sits here and tries to run my life. Whenever I take a good look at it, I begin to think that even the karma between people and objects can be adverse. So I perceive the clock as being more than just a clock on a desk; it also frequently serves as an impediment.

One morning last winter, as soon as I returned from morning homage at the main temple, I sensed that a thief had been in my room while I was gone. I had never been in the habit of locking the door so anyone could just walk in. I looked around the room and realized that he had taken only the things I needed for everyday life. He evidently needed exactly the same things that I did.

He left behind much more than he took. But the fact that I had things to lose in the first place—that is, to think that I had something that someone else might covet—was more than a small embarrassment for me. However, objects are not things that I hoard for myself. They're things that come to me through karma. And since I believe that they leave me when that karma is over, I have no regrets about losing them. If I consider that perhaps in a former life I stole something equivalent to my loss and that this loss was retribution—what goes around comes around—then I feel quite lighthearted by having paid off a karmic debt.

But the thief must have thought that there was something really valuable in my room since he turned the place inside out and upside down. I wasn't a bit sad about losing anything, but, as I put back several scattered pieces of clothing one by one, I started to feel a new sense of sadness about the human condition.

Soon, however, the first thing I missed more than anything else was the desk clock. So a few days later I went out to buy another one.

I decided that instead of getting a flashy new one that might tempt another thief, I'd buy a secondhand one so I went to one of those shops downtown with secondhand goods. And as soon as I stepped in the door, alas, alas, alas, there was my stolen desk clock just sitting there waiting for me. A young fellow, who apparently had brought the clock in after taking it from my room, and the owner were haggling over it.

As soon as the young fellow saw me, he blushed and turned away, trying to hide his embarrassment. And I was just as embarrassed for him.

Finally, in giving the young fellow a few coins, I wound up buying back my own clock. I was not about to pose as a personification of magnanimity anxious to forgive him, because, if you really think about it, as people we all have a lot of similar shortcomings in this life. Who knows, I probably would be capable of doing the same thing if circumstances demanded it. I was grateful just to have the unexpected karma of meeting the clock again, so I simply tried to retain my own composure for his sake as well as for my own.

I like to think that genuine forgiveness, rather than being some self-styled act of benevolence, is the art of keeping your wits together and considering the karma involved. *(1972)*

22. Survivors

Just in the last couple of days, busy splotches of green that had hidden themselves in late fall have been spreading about the fields and it's fascinating to watch these new neighbors break through the earth. As if recognizing their chance to show off, these hibernating patches of green are gathering together and springing up to once again announce themselves and the new season.

I fertilized plants around my hut with chicken droppings that I had gotten a few days earlier at a nearby village. Soon that awful stench will be traveling up from the roots to the stems, and then down the branches and into buds in a startling transformation from stench to fragrance. One can't help but admire the earth's balancing harmonies.

To smell the earth in the early spring is to fill the heart with the joy of life, and to feel the earth in the fields under your bare feet is to feel the maternal warmth of nature.

While digging into the soil to lay some fertilizer, I suddenly became conscious of the fact that I was a survivor. I once again realized that I hadn't been buried yet. I'm still here. We're not usually conscious of this as we go about our lives.

That thought first occurred to me last fall on a bus. I had been given a seat at the very back beside the emergency exit. As we passed a huge public cemetery that was as jam-packed with the dead as the bus was with the living, I became conscious of the fact that I was, after all, still alive, a survivor.

Even if I hadn't become conscious of this by seeing a cemetery while riding on a passing bus, it is true that all of us alive today are survivors. But we never know when our time will be up. Our lives are at the mercy of the wheels of the bus, should the driver glance the wrong way even for a second. Nightly, poisonous gas from the charcoal briquettes could leak through cracks in the floor as we sleep. There are an endless number of diseases, wartime massacres, unexpected disasters, and our own inner conflicts. We are all really lucky survivors in this chasm of danger called "life."

What makes us so sad about death, more than it being an eternal parting, is the loss of life. Life is such a very precious end in itself. For someone to consider it simply as a means to an end is an absolute, irrevocable evil. The unforgivable evil of war, even if it were considered morally justifiable at the time, is the compunctionless slaughter of innumerable precious and innocent lives.

Thus, as survivors we have an obligation to really take care of one another. And as survivors we have an additional obligation to at least live our lives to the utmost, if for no other reason than for those who lost their lives prematurely. We should constantly reflect upon whether or not we are living up to those obligations.

When I lived near the city, whenever I came upon the tired eyes of people at night returning home after a hard day's work, I wanted to greet each one of them with a hearty, "We've survived another day!"

And so, as a survivor myself, I fertilized the freshly sprouting plants, plants that had survived the freezing winter. One way or another, we're all survivors. *(1972)*

23. A Change of Heart

If I had my own way, I'd just become a leisurely man of enlightenment, without a thing to bother me. But, since that is not the case, I have to live like all other sentient beings amidst contradictions and conflicts. However, if we look closely, we find that our anger and frustrations and resentments are not caused by outside stimuli; rather, they're caused by our own lack of self-control when reacting to outside stimuli.

A couple of years ago, some of the bureaucratic monks at the sect headquarters sold off a portion of the farmland that belonged to the temple where I was staying at the time. I was so angry I could hardly sleep for a number of nights. The land was sold against the consensus of the sect as a whole and it had been carried out on the sly. I could barely control myself when I saw hundreds of pines being felled and bulldozers tearing the mountain apart.

It was during that period that everything seemed to be going against me, resulting in an all-pervading resentment. Even the temple master, who had kind of kept me under his wing, had gone to direct another temple, leaving me like an orphan. I was in the process of making up my mind to pack up and leave as well, to move to another temple, and to forget everything.

Then one morning, on my way back down the mountain after the predawn chanting at the Main Buddha Hall, an old saying suddenly came to mind:

"Nothing ever existed."

And the second I thought about that, all of my resentment melted away instantly.

Of course! Nothing ever existed! We have nothing when we're born and nothing when we die. We simply follow our karma, and when the karma is over, we just dissipate and transform into something else. Sooner or later, we all have to leave behind our bodies. Nothing has ever existed as a permanent, unchanging, independent entity.

Once I started thinking in these terms, I experienced a major change of heart toward everything. Since I wasn't about to become a temple master, it didn't really matter where I lived, for the experience, as a regular monk would be basically the same no matter where I went. It's the same in the secular world as well: It really doesn't matter where you live, since the same problems will always be with you regardless of the surroundings. And, if that is so, then all of our problems simply depend on how we regard them. So I decided to stay where I was and learn to grow in such an unfavorable situation rather than trying to flee it. There's an old adage that if you fall on the ground, you have to push against the ground to get back up.

So I stopped fretting over the land. Actually, it wasn't the temple's land in the first place. Perhaps a devotee had donated it or perhaps there never had been an owner and the temple had just taken it over. The land was just following its own karma. Just because the temple sold it didn't mean that the land had disappeared. It just changed owners.

From that day on, I felt calm and collected and I started sleeping well again. The sounds of the bulldozers and the jackhammers didn't bother me at all anymore, since I had changed my entire way of thinking.

I had often told others to be kind and generous, but how kind and generous had I been myself? The sounds of the jackhammers and bulldozers weren't there intentionally to disturb our sleep. They were there to make room to build homes for people without homes. Why shouldn't I listen to the noise from that perspective?

And there were hundreds of workers at the site working around the clock. Each of them no doubt had a family to feed, perhaps a relative in a hospital, and school payments to make for a child or two. They also had to buy fuel to warm their homes, and they had the added cost of having winter kimchi made before the snow started flying. Plus all the other responsibilities of a family man. When I really thought about it, how could I ever have complained so self-centeredly about the noise?

After considering things from this vein, the noise didn't bother me at all. It was from then on that my thoughts and values started to change dramatically. It really hit home that this was not my world, that the world didn't exist to please me, and that we all have to live in this world together.

Naturally, I also gained a new perspective on ownership and loss. Since there is nothing I can claim as my own, I can't lose anything. And if there were something that I did lose, it would be a gain for someone else, so a loss followed by a gain meant nothing lost.

Occasionally, thieves come into temples, for temples, too, are subject to the ways of the world. There are even thieves who "patronize" the same temple from time to time, taking advantage of the lack of security to help "air the place out." Previously, whenever I lost possessions in such cases, I was both disappointed and resentful. But realizing that nothing ever existed, that is, that ultimately nothing is ever ours and that everything is impermanent, I dropped those attitudes. I felt that I had just passed things, which had been under my care for a while, on to others. If you watch closely, it seems that things, too, have their own karma.

There are times when we can't even be sure of our own minds. They can be the subtlest yet most capricious things in the world. When we're feeling generous, we accept everything that comes along with a smile, but when we close our minds, there's not even room for a needle to squeeze in. And to have a change of heart is not an easy thing to accomplish.

But I alone am responsible for the way I think and feel. In overcoming anger, there are of course external circumstances to be considered, but learning how to make an internal change of heart is training that we all need.

So finally I understood why in the old days people said that it's more important to master your heart than to just follow it. *(1972)*

24. A Book One Summer

Everyone has pegged autumn as the season for reading, but personally I think it's the worst season of all for books. That's because the weather is so clear and perfect. Since the lengthening shadows of the trees beckon us to hit the road, wasting time leafing through the pages of a book under such a beautiful blue sky seems ridiculous. It's being rude to the fantastic fall weather.

Also, the notion that there has to be a separate season for reading is ridiculous. The season to read is whenever you feel like reading. Actually the summer isn't a bad time, since the humidity's often too stifling to spend much time outdoors. Up in the mountains it's the perfect time to spread out a mat and stretch out in some light clothes with a ventilated bamboo pillow. And there's no need to go to the trouble of finding some secluded place. All you have to do is just use your imagination and invite the rolling ocean and the flowing valley streams to join you and to cool you off.

One year I forgot the heat of the summer by reading and reciting the "Ten Dedications" section from the Avatamsaka (Garland) Sutra. Previously, I had been greatly moved by both a monk's lecture on the sutra and by Samantabhadra's (the Bodhisattva of Universal Practice) fervent seeking of truth in that section of the sutra. I made up my mind that someday I would get around to reading it carefully. The time was ripe that summer at Haeinsa Temple, so I did.

Mornings and evenings I went up to the Repository of *Tripitaka Koreana*, the Korean Buddhist Canon, and did regular repentance practice to cleanse away unfavorable karma. I spent the rest of each day immersed in the "Ten Dedications" chapter of the sutra in my room.

The tiny room I had was terribly confining. There was only a skylight looking down from the rafters, and a single door, making the room suffocating in any season. But as if to compensate, there was a good view of the mountain across the way. As I looked out from the room with the door flung open, the doorframe also served as a picture frame for a beautiful painting of nature.

So everyday I put on my formal robes, lit some incense, sat properly, opened the chapter, and first recited the "Chant for Opening a Sutra":

So auspicious to come across such deep and mystical
Dharma teachings even once in fathomless eons!
Thus may I read them and listen to them and recite them
in order to know the Tathagata's true meaning.

I read the version translated into Chinese by Siksananda (652-710CE) and printed from the *Tripitaka Koreana* woodblocks at Haeinsa. Even though it has been translated into Korean, there was something very special about the lingering imagery from reading the Chinese ideograms printed from the woodblocks, something incomparably serene—a visually induced tranquility. At times I recited out loud and at times I just read silently.

On really humid days, the stench from the outhouse wafted over the wall. Whenever it bothered me, I just considered the fact that I had my own personal latrine within me and that, after all, I, too, had contributed to that stench over there myself. I also considered the fact that the physical stench from the outhouse wasn't as bad as the stench of someone betraying his own conscience. So it became easy to overcome the initial displeasure about the malodorous outhouse. Everything depends on how you look at it.

Every day I'd finish reading about an hour before the evening meal and when I arose, the floor cushion would be soaked from the sweat that had seeped through my robes. That's when I realized how really hot it was. I was so absorbed in reading that the heat hadn't bothered me. So I'd go out to the stream and soak my clothes in it. I'd cool off immediately and feel light and refreshed. And I'd be overcome with a feeling of gratitude for everything.

That is how I spent the entire summer, reading and reciting "Ten Dedications" at least ten times. And each time I reread and recited it, each word, each sentence seemed to take on a new and more profound meaning. That probably wouldn't have been the case had I been ordered to read it by someone else, but since it was something I just wanted to do, I was able to reap its true joy.

But what exactly is reading, if not hearing your own original voice through somebody else's? *(1972)*

25. Rust Corrodes Iron

I wonder if there's anything more baffling than the human heart. When people are in a good mood, they accept the whole world with open arms; but once they close their hearts, there's not even room for a needle. That seems to be our nature, which no doubt accounts for the popularity of the song lyrics, "I don't even know my own heart." It sounds irresponsible, but as simple as it is, it's a truth beyond refute: Sometimes we don't even know our own hearts.

Take the workplace for example, where human relations are extremely important. Sometimes we have a good day even with just a nod from someone, while on another day just seeing the shadow of someone else can ruin everything. Often enough when people reflect on why they left a job, it's very likely has it has something to do with interpersonal relationships.

It's so strange that the same heart can like one person and detest another. From some religious interpretations, this can be attributed to prior karma, and even from a common sense point of view, there has to be à reason somewhere. Results necessarily follow causes.

Even so, we have to compromise a lot to make the best of our work relations. We should be grateful for the karma of meeting at a common workplace. Probabilities aren't very high of working at the same place in Seoul, a city of over six million; in the southern half of a divided Korea, a peninsula with over fifty million inhabitants; in Asia, a huge and hugely populated continent; and on a planet with well over three billion people. From this perspective, we should indeed be grateful for having met anyone at all.

Even if something that someone does disgusts us, we have no choice but to have a change of heart and accept it. If we hate someone else, we actually hate ourselves. If we continue to live our lives filled with disgust and hate, we are the ones who eventually suffer. To hate is to suffer. Living each day this way does nothing but stain our hearts.

So we should take our interpersonal relationships as opportunities to learn about life and to cleanse our hearts. We have to deepen the meaning of our own lives by having a change of heart whenever we need one.

Sooner or later knots have to be untied. If we don't untie them in this life, then who knows when we'll be able to. So employment is more than just a good opportunity in itself; a workplace provides us with the opportunity to strengthen our powers of friendship and kindness. The greatness of work lies in the fact that it brings people together. It is through work that we can come together and bond, that we come to understand others, and that we overcome our petty likes and dislikes. Everything depends on how we handle our hearts.

Even monastic life and discipline depend entirely on the heart, and that's because heart is the basis of everything. We find a metaphor in the Dhammapada Sutra: "Iron gives birth to rust, but that rust proceeds to eat the iron away." So, in the same sense, if we cast shadows on our hearts, those shadows begin to corrode us like rust corrodes iron.

If we wish to become genuinely warm people, we have to know how to use our hearts. And that doesn't happen by chance. We have to learn how through our daily interactions. Why do we have to dislike or hate one another? Aren't we all the same wayfarers on the same boat heading in the same direction? *(1973)*

Part II:
What More Could You Want?

26. Eternal Mountains

You might laugh if I told you that there are people in the mountains who are nostalgic for the mountains. But it's true. Monks' nostalgia for the mountains is so strong that it makes them rush to them. Even if a monk lives on one mountain, he becomes nostalgic for one that he used to live on. And he also dreams about ones that he has only heard about and hasn't been to.

A local dictionary defines a mountain as "a part of the earth that is higher than its surrounding terrain." This conceptualization of a mountain draws a chuckle from us mountain people, since it sounds like a sentence for a written exam or an abstract description of a mountain.

A mountain is more than just a bulge that sticks out of the earth. It is also deep valleys. It is trees and boulders and streams and all kinds of birds. It is beasts and fog and fish and frogs and clouds and wind and rumblings. Yet it's more than just an ecosystem. It is also decaying ancient temples and makeshift huts and a zillion other things. And people live on it.

There's a saying that people live in the mountains because they like them. And it's true that people who don't like mountains can't live there. It's also true that once you live in the mountains you become so attached that you can't just pick up and leave.

Every time we monks step out of a mountain temple gate, the mountains offer us something new. This is particularly true when summer has turned to fall, a time when mountains thrill the hearts of the monks, who are the mountains' eternal servants. The changing colors of the foliage tell us that it's time for wild grapes and Asian kiwi and akebi berries. So as soon as the daily routine ends on autumnal afternoons—it doesn't matter whether it's meditation or sutra study or whatever—the temples empty. Everyone heads for the fruit vines, just like the rest of the creatures in the forests. Wild chestnuts fall in great numbers and nothing could be sweeter to the ear than that familiar sound echoing through the valleys. Such things are part of what makes mountain people mountain people.

In the old days a temple monk who tired of the mountain where he lived would leave his colleagues and head deeper into the mountains to be by himself. There he'd set up a small thatched hut and without a single possession he'd befriend nature as he strove for enlightenment.

> A small thatched hut among a bunch of clouds,
> Free to sit and recline and stroll at will.
> The cold stream sings of wisdom,
> The fresh breeze and the moon satiate completely.

This type of elegant refrain could come not only from its author, Goryeo Kingdom National Zen Master Naong, but from anyone who knows the mountains and the Way. Being deep in the mountains, you're free from the shadows of others and free to forget everything. Free to close off the world with a three- or four-foot door made of branches. Free to sleep when tired, to eat when hungry, and to live without a care. But it's not just to escape the secular world and to live as a hermit. It's a course in silence until the time comes when one can roar forth the mighty words of enlightenment.

My small hermitage on the edge of the city is like a bit of paradise: It has some woods and birds and a lotus pond. But on a sultry summer's day, I suddenly think of the mountains and I get sick inside just longing for the sound of a stream. However, no longer are there many pristine mountains left to dash off to. Even the really secluded areas are quickly disappearing under the banners of tourism. When I realize that, once again I have to fold in my wings.

The real monks are fleeing deeper and deeper into the mountains. They're fleeing the great mountain temples now filled with tourists just like the birds are fleeing the cities now filled with pollution. *(1973)*

27. Standing under a Tree

A lot of people look quite fine by themselves. But people start to look rather shabby when standing under a large, healthy tree. In comparison, trees are absolutely magnificent.

As people, we have so very much to learn from trees. I think it's rather embarrassing to us as humans when we compare our behavior to the discipline, natural order, and adaptability of trees.

When a violent storm strikes, birds chirping on the ends of branches suddenly take off to find a place of shelter. People bring in their shoes, shut their doors and windows tightly, and pull the curtains shut. But trees just stand there to meet the storm. And they adjust to the fact that sometimes leaves and branches get torn off and broken in the winds. We should bow our heads in respect to the resoluteness of these trees that bow to the wind.

When rain falls the urban alleyways fill with people under umbrellas, with each person walking rather glumly under one. Occasionally there may be two people under an umbrella but the umbrellas of the secular world are so narrow they hardly cover a single person's shoulders. That reflects how stingy space and urban life have become.

Cities have become so crowded that not only do we step on our own shadows; we are losing even the shade of our own hearts. And there is not a single thing for us to lean against, like a tree. We can't help but feel shabby and embarrassed compared to a tree, a tree that lets birds nest on its branches, a tree that provides enough cool shade to embrace scores and sometimes even hundreds of people, a tree that serves as a giant umbrella, a tree that let's you lean against it.

At Haeinsa Temple there's a cluster of fir trees hundreds of years old, with one in particular shooting up above the others. But if you look closely at the base of that tree, you notice that people have etched their names all over as high as they could possibly reach. How could people, who dread their own aging, have no compunctions about scarring an aging tree? Did the tree commit some kind of crime? All it did was cast cool shadows upon the earth on hot summer days and sing songs of transience with the wind.

People even go so far as to carve their names on that fir tree to demonstrate their importance. But just across the way from that tree stands the repository for Tripitaka Koreana, which is comprised of 81,258 woodblocks carved in the thirteenth century. Yes, 81,258 woodblocks. Yet not a single signature can be found on any one of those woodblocks, no matter how hard you look. We haven't a single clue as to who carved the more than fifty million Chinese ideograms onto them. The artisans just selflessly carved what had to be carved. That is how humble and virtuous the people of yesteryear were. So when I stand beneath a fir tree with names carved all over it, I once again feel shabby and embarrassed as a human being, and I feel sorry for the tree.

Most people become gentle when they stand under a tree. People who just a short time ago were conniving amid an environment of concrete walls and asphalt can no longer do so when standing under the gentleness of a tree. Their voices become soft as they talk of eternal joys, and they ponder the nature of goodness and truth. And they begin to become faintly aware of their daily lives of busily running about in their crowded urban cubicles of noise and pollution.

When you look at it that way, you can see that human beings don't belong in an exhausting urban environment of noise and dust. You come to realize that people belong to the remarkable natural embroidery of trees and birds and waters and clouds and stars. The fact that humanity's great religions and philosophies were born out of secluded nature and not out of walls of concrete and brick gives credence to this.

Can people really dare say that nature is something to be conquered? On the contrary, we have so very much to learn from nature's order and humility and virtue. *(1973)*

28. The Limits of Knowledge

On occasion, knowledge tires me out. If I have a long talk with well educated people, the only thing I get out of it is weariness. Of course there is much to learn, and new things to hear and become aware of, but doctrines and theories by distinguished scholars are not of particular relevance to my daily existence.

Theories on etymology and morphology can sometimes lead us into valleys of meaninglessness. Knowledge that is highly complicated and refractive can blind us rather than make us see, since such knowledge blocks the potential of intuition and creativity. As a result, I generally don't give much credence to empty, vague theories that exclude personal experiences.

Truth should be plain and simple. And it should be expressed in simple terms to make it comprehensible to everybody. So it baffles me as to why people have to go to such an extent to apply so many complicated theories when speaking of truth. In addition, there is also the world of truth that cannot even be expressed in words. The arrogant blind spot of knowledge is its attempt to explain the infinite in finite words.

In ninth-century China, there was a renowned sutra scholar-monk named Teshan. He was particularly well versed in the Diamond Sutra and, as a result of his expert lectures on the subject, he became known as "Diamond Chou." "Chou" had been his family name before he became a monk.

At the time Zen was taking hold in regions south of the Yangtze River. Master Teshan believed that people could only realize their Buddha nature through endless eons of scripture study and that Zen "attaining Buddhahood by pointing directly to the mind" was nonsense. So he took it upon himself to go south and teach the Zen people in the south this truth of his. He packed his knapsack and left that very day.

A few days later as he journeyed south, he came across a rice cake shop and he stopped to look. The old woman selling the cakes asked him, "What do you have in that knapsack?"

He answered quite proudly, "Commentaries on the Diamond Sutra."

The old woman spoke again. "Well, according to the Diamond Sutra, you can't grasp past mind, present mind, or future mind. So how are you going to eat rice cakes?"

He couldn't answer.

"With your mouth!" said the woman.

Teshan was dumbfounded. He had been so proud of his knowledge and scholarly efforts on the Diamond Sutra, yet a simple country grandmother selling rice cakes had put him down. He realized that he had become an expert on theory but lacked wisdom.

Following the directions of the rice cake seller, and with her wisdom in mind, Teshan continued to head south to Dragon Pond Temple. When he arrived he bellowed out, "I've heard so much about Dragon Pond Temple; but, having arrived, I see neither a dragon nor a pond."

An old monk in tattered robes stepped out and said, "You have already been to Dragon Pond yourself." (You have already seen your Buddha nature.)

Teshan was once again speechless.

Teshan and the old monk, Zen Master Lungtan, talked late into the night. Finally Master Lungtan suggested that they retire. Teshan stepped out to go to the guest quarters and said that it was so dark he couldn't see a thing. So the old monk handed him a candle and as Teshan reached for it, Master Lungtan blew it out. Whence upon Teshan became enlightened.

The following day, Teshan burnt all of the commentaries on the Diamond Sutra that he had so carefully brought south on his back. Although the written word in itself is not necessarily useless, he burned the commentaries because he felt that they had only fooled him.

This is how people make really strong bonds with each other—through wisdom rather than through knowledge. *(1973)*

29. Finding Principles in Work

A fellow who had come to the temple a couple of months ago to become a monk left this morning. He said that he decided to leave because he had found the routine too difficult. There's a saying in temples that we shouldn't stop anyone from coming or hold back anyone from leaving, so we didn't try to prevent him from going back down the hill.

Evidently he had the idea that he would come to the temple, become a monk, and sit around smelling the pine breezes and taking it easy. He had no idea that just eating and lolling around are totally against monastic regulations.

On the contrary, there's a very strong rule that when there's a collective project, everyone comes out and works together. Sometimes, however, the younger monks feel bad watching the old monks working so hard alongside them. Yet the older monks won't listen if the younger monks suggest that they go back and rest. Once, feeling sorry for an old monk, a young monk took his tool and hid it; if you don't have a tool, you can't come out and work. The strategy was successful: The older monk couldn't find his tool so he didn't come out to work that day. And the older monk didn't appear at mealtime, either. It was then that the younger monk realized the very literal meaning of the temple saying that if you don't work a day, you don't eat. This is a universal principle throughout the community of monks.

It's also common practice throughout the community to give all of the dirty work to the new novices. But the purpose is not to just give them a rough time and use them to the hilt. The real meaning is to have them make progress on the Path by bearing hardships and learning the importance of patience. Everyone suffers a few nosebleeds when doing strenuous work that they're not used to. Although abstract theories are meaningless to someone who leaves the temple because he can't take it physically, we can in fact learn new principles through hard work, and that is precisely where we find foundations for new development and growth.

Once, a master told a novice to replace the earthen brace for a cauldron that sat over the fire pit. Although the novice lacked the skills, he tried his best the first time. He even smoothed out the earthen rim as best he could to hold the cauldron perfectly in place. But when his master came and inspected the job, he told him to do it over again. The novice thought that he had done a good job but since he couldn't disobey his teacher, he knocked down the whole thing and started over. The teacher came again, inspected, and said that the cauldron was tilted slightly and told him to do it again.

The novice wound up redoing the cauldron setting a total of nine times. Usually a novice might have to redo it a couple of times, catch some flack, and leave it at that. But by having to redo it nine times, the novice had no choice but to really learn how to hold his temper and to learn patience and forbearance. In the process, he was also able to realize his teacher's genuine intent. The novice's determination to silently accept the order to replace the cauldron so many times no doubt influenced his ability to become a prominent Zen master later in life.

The life of a monk is not to be found outside of his daily routines. Sutra study and meditation are no more than attempts to improve our daily lives, which might otherwise become filled with contradictions and conflicts. The saying that the Way is to be found in ordinary life supports this.

A person who is too quick or too lazy in his work cannot succeed in the other monastic practices, be it sutra study, praying, chanting or meditating, because these other activities are all done with the same heart. Learning a principle from work and applying it to everything is the best way for a practitioner to approach his study. *(1973)*

30. To New Practitioners

We often call renunciation "leaving home and entering the mountains" since it is the process of leaving family and friends and entering a temple to become a monk. This renunciation is also the process of leaving the world of attachments and never looking back, but that is not a very easy thing to do. It might be easier to do in an instant on a single thought, but usually it takes several failures and disappointments in secular life to foster a mind conducive to renunciation. In addition, of all those who come to join the temple, there are many who never really find themselves; and sometimes there are new practitioners whose shadow of the past follows them up the mountain to the temple and eventually leads them back down again.

To adjust to life as a practitioner, first a person has to change all of his notions. It is absolutely essential that he replace worldly perceptions with those of a practitioner. There are many Buddhist books about how to go about this, as well as other catalysts to be found in Tripitaka Koreana and other renowned scriptures. Perhaps the best book for a new novice is the Dhammapada.

The Dhammapada is an exquisite collection of Buddhist truths in poetic form. It is not a separate single work but rather a collection of 305 of the Buddha's talks compiled into a total of 423 verses in twenty six chapters. The contents are highly practical, accessible, and relevant to our daily lives.

It is an excellent book for a beginner since it centers on basic Buddhist ethics. As a result, it has always been a greatly loved work of poetry recited by Buddhists everywhere. Compiled around the third and second centuries BCE, it is one of the earliest sutras to have been recorded.

*****

Even as rain penetrates
A poorly thatched house,
So does lust penetrate
An undeveloped mind.
Mind is the forerunner of all evil states.
Mind is chief; mind-made the evil states are.
If one speaks or acts with a wicked mind,
Suffering follows him as inexorably
As the cartwheels follow the hooves of the ox.

It is really difficult for us to know our true heart. When we're feeling good, we're ready to accept everything, but once we close our hearts, there's not even room enough for a pin.

It is precisely this heart that is the greatest issue in Buddhism. Buddhism considers it foolish to seek anything outside of one's own heart, outside of oneself. And we become warmer people when we reach the point where can control our hearts as we wish. That is why we always say it's best to control your heart rather than to just follow it. If we just follow our hearts, they sway with fleeting impulses and this is precisely what we have to control. People who have renounced the world lose the true meaning of their practice if they do not learn how to control their hearts.

*****

If, as the disciple fares along,
He meets no companion who is better or equal,
Let him firmly pursue his solitary career.
This is better than fellowship with the foolish.

We frequently say that there are three things that are necessary for the new novice to practice properly: He has to meet the right teacher, the right fellow practitioners, and the right temple. Among these three, the role of fellow practitioners is of great importance. Virtuous practitioners can be a great influence but foolish practitioners can ruin other's practice without even realizing it. The influence of friends, whether good or bad, is like something hiding in the fog that slowly but inexorably dampens you.

The statement that it is better to go it alone if you don't have any helpful friends is referring directly to your determination and attitudes. In reality, the life of a practitioner is a solitary one. There is no one who can solve a practitioner's problems for him. It is essential that he overcome and resolve the problems himself. A solitary life in the secular world is in fact a lonely one, but for a practitioner time spent alone can be worthwhile. If a person can't endure such time alone as a practitioner, then there's no need to continue on. If a practitioner becomes irresolute, then he'll wind up an eternal wanderer, neither a monk nor a layperson. One should realize that being alone, rather than being something idyllic or romantic, is a difficult yet dignified human existence that a practitioner must constantly experience.

*****

Consort not with those who are dear
And never with those who are not dear.
Not seeing those who are dear
And seeing those who are not dear
Are both painful.

Hence hold nothing dear, for separation
From those who are dear is painful;
Such bonds do not exist for those
Who hold nothing dear or not dear.

The point here is to restrict secular affections. Most of our conflicts derive from human relationships and you don't have to read society columns day and night to realize that. Our dissatisfaction is the result of being bound to something or someone. And the strings of love are tough and strong enough to blind even a flawless person. If a practitioner becomes entangled that way just once, he can wind up completely lost, not even knowing his own heart, as a popular song goes. Peace of mind can come only from going beyond affection. Love in the community of monks does not mean being bound to one another; rather, it is looking after one another with a sense of freedom. Rather than looking at each other, we look in the same direction together. *(1973)*

31. The Meaning of Silence

We're living at a time when people talk and talk and talk. The basic functions of the mouth were to eat and to spit but today's mouths are having a rough life, working overtime as they spit out a lot of unnecessary jabber. In the old days people talked to each other face-to-face, but now, since the advent of telephones and then electronics, people can talk to their heart's content without even seeing another person. The irony is that even though we talk more, we seem to be saying less.

We spend our days, except for the time by ourselves, making noise over nothing. We should be saying only what we have to say and saying things that are true; so it's rather disheartening to observe how we spend so much time just blabbering away. Haven't you ever felt like you've actually cheated yourself a little by saying something trivial or irrelevant?

Once in awhile I think about how to recognize a really good friend. You can recognize one first by whether or not you're really aware of the time you spend together. It's not a friend if spending time together is a chore. Rather, it's a friend if the time flies by before you realize it, because spending time with a real friend is beyond time and space. We can experience the same thing when we pray or chant. When the prayers are going really well, we transcend time and space, but when they're not going so well, we become conscious of time and space, and praying becomes nothing more than an empty exercise.

How else can we recognize a friend? Real friends can spend time together without even talking. It's like romping about a field together without opening your mouth. Real friends can communicate continuously and preciously without saying a single word. At that level, they have transcended time and space.

Talk always carries with it the potential for misunderstandings. Sometimes there are even misunderstandings when the same thing is expressed two ways, since the people involved may not understand the real or subtle meaning. Yet mothers can understand their unintelligible children merely through vibrations. In this way loves grows out of silence.

Talk not born out of a background of silence is nothing but static. You can tell the limits of our language by just listening to people rattle on. The talk that comes pouring out of our mouths nowadays is becoming rougher and cruder and meaner, which indicates the extent to which we have become shabbier inside. That's because we aren't accepting the light of silence from within.

So many people nowadays are in such a rush, they've forgotten how to talk for themselves. They just mimic politicians, singers, and comedians, and consequently they've lost any sense of discretion. In this process, they are loosing the ability to even think for themselves.

In regard to the virtue of religious reticence, through meditation and contemplation we come to hear the language inside of us. That sound is unedited and unadulterated holy scripture. Isn't the purpose of reading religious scriptures to become capable of understanding words that haven't even been printed yet, and to live by those words? To quote a Buddhist sutra:

Each person has his own sutra
But not one on paper or in print.
When you open it up, there's not a single character,
Just an eternally bright light.

In our daily lives, we spend our time trying to recognize only that which we can see, hear, and hold in our hands. But there really is something as invisible and inaudible and elusive as silence. Once you free yourself from your own fixed ideas, a bright light begins to shine in your unfettered heart.

Small signs with the words "total silence" are placed inside and outside temple meditation halls. Talking only serves as an impediment to progress to those involved in meditation. Disputes invariably arise in communal life, and once people start arguing, they lose their concentration. Meditation requires pure concentration and a complete look into oneself. You have to go beyond the world of arguments and discrimination if you are to step into the world of complete absorption.

Talk is touted as a means of communication but sometimes it can have the opposite effect, and the old saying that "the mouth is the door to disaster" reflects such possibilities. Some Zen monks are spending three, even ten years in total silence. No one dares to speak to them.

Religious people don't remain silent for the sake of silence. It's a filtration process to listen to real talk, and to develop the ability to speak fairly and truthfully through the light of silence. This is where we find the difference between a true practitioner of silence and a deaf mute.

Kahlil Gibran wrote that he learned silence from the talkative, and listening from the inner ear. The utmost language is, in fact, silence. Yet there are times when people have to say what has to be said. There are times when some people insist on silence even when they should be saying something. In such a case, silence is not a virtue. Such silence at times smells of criminality. To remain silent when right should be distinguished from wrong is nothing more than a cowardly way out.

Silence isn't meant to be cowardly silence. Silence provides us with the opportunity to learn to speak fairly and truthfully rather than frivolously. Yet only totally candid people can really speak fairly and truthfully. By uniting people, including religious people, who can speak in such a way, we can dig our way out of a dark tunnel and into a brighter world. *(1974)*

32. A Rat

It's late August and the autumn winds are already starting to ride their way into the mountain temples. The humidity and stickiness of the morning summer breezes are being replaced in the afternoons with perfectly dry ones. Suddenly I can feel the breath of fall.

This is the time of year when the three-month summer meditation season ends, the monks all take off, and the temples are practically empty. Collard doves descend upon the empty fields to peck for food while squirrels come up to play on the back porch. Perhaps because they didn't have a full chance to display their powers in the summer, thunder and lightning arrive to ransack the ravines. Feeling a bit chilly, I light a fire in the morning and evening, and it's time once again to put away the cool hemp clothes of summer. A casual glance at the mountain across the way from the hermitage reveals a hitherto unnoticed change of color, the beginnings of a kind of haggard, wasted look.

Once when I was staying at a secluded hermitage about this time of year, the meditation season ended and my fellow monks descended the mountain, leaving me totally alone. In those days the general public was so busy just trying to make ends meet, they didn't have the luxury of going hiking or sightseeing. So the entire area was totally deserted, and the days were very uneventful—days when, even if you set a pot of water on the brazier to boil, there was no one around to share a cup of tea. The only sign of life was an occasional villager who would come up the mountain to pick wild herbs.

One day after finishing my meal, as usual I took some food to put atop a boulder out back. That was where we placed food offerings, as is Buddhist custom, for any hungry sentient beings that might be around. That particular day there was a rat sitting there. Since he didn't budge when he saw me, I figured that he was waiting for a meal. His presence explained why the area around the boulder had been so clean all summer. Usually it's the birds and squirrels who eat the offerings and make a mess, although on occasion the next day the food is still there, completely untouched. But more often than not during the summer, the area was completely clean. Now I understood that it was this rat who had been dining.

Since I was having only one meal a day, it was around noontime that I went out with the food offering. Inevitably the rat would be there waiting right on schedule. Previously, even just the sight of a rat's tail used to give me goose bumps, but in that isolation in the mountains I was happy to see even a rat. And since this little sentient being had become dependent upon me, I developed a special feeling for him. Sometimes I even gave him more than I ate myself. And he soon grew noticeably larger, about three times his original size.

Every day I would come out and say, "You're here again! Well, come and eat!" As soon as I'd put the food down, he would come over my way and eat to his heart's content. In this way we tamed each other.

One day I had decided that I had something I wanted to say to the rat. As usual, he came over and ate. I waited until he finished before speaking to him.

"Well, Mr. Rat, if you, too, have a spirit, then listen to me. That dreadful guise that you're wearing is the result of lifetimes of unfavorable karma. But this time around, you've come to this pure place of Dharma practice, and spending time here with me is good for you. It's good karma for you to hang out at a hermitage. So please get rid of that awful guise, come back in your next life in a better form, and achieve eternal liberation. How long do you have to stand around dressed like that? Liberate yourself! Namu Amitabul!"

The rat had sat there listening intently to the whole thing. Then he waddled away.

The next day when I took out the food offering, the rat was nowhere to be seen. I wondered what could be wrong. Then I looked down and saw him splayed out in front of the boulder, dead.

In today's world, often there's no real communication between people, whether because of distrust or disinterest or dislike. Thus, a rat listening to someone is something really quite remarkable. This confirmed for me over and over again that even though we all have different guises, all sentient beings have the exact same basic desire to live gently.

I did some chanting and buried the rat right there in front of the boulder. But as I continued to wish the rat well every day in the following months, I couldn't help but feel, deep down inside, tinges of sadness and impermanence from the dry, hollow autumn winds. *(1974)*

33. Silent Promises

In a secular world that is becoming increasingly complex and heartless, we are becoming bound by such a sea of laws that we can hardly keep track of them. It's difficult to understand why we need so many laws and regulations just to get on with our lives. When powerful laws are enacted and proclaimed, you would think that life would become smoother, but it seems that actually the opposite is happening, with more sensational and horrible crimes increasing day by day. We can't help but envy the people of yesteryear who got by so well without so many laws.

When you're walking in the mountains and you come to a fork in the path, you'll often see indicators made from rock piles or branches to lead you the right way. It's then that we become aware of the debt of gratitude we owe to the gentle people who set up the signs for us. They show us the right path without written or spoken words. These indicators, far from restricting us, make us both happy and grateful. Even promises, when based on such humanistic trust, are sacred.

Once my teacher Zen Master Hyobong told me a story about when he was a young monk "floating like the clouds and flowing like the waters," as we call traveling around freely between meditation retreats. Someone told him about a silent, nearly timeless promise handed down through the ages at a particular hermitage. The hermitage was high in the mountains and few people came around, so a meditator had an ideal environment for the summer meditation retreat. But by mid-October that monk would have to hurry down the mountain or be stranded until the following spring because the snow would soon be piling high.

When a monk first arrived at the hermitage for the summer retreat, he would find a full supply of food and firewood so that he could pass the retreat in worry-free comfort. In the fall, after the retreat was over and before the snow started flying, he would go down to the villages below the mountain to collect food offerings, and then come back and replenish supplies and firewood for whoever came next. If he came back to the hermitage a few years later, there might be traces of someone having been there, but food and firewood supplies would be as perfectly stocked as if no one had touched them.

Of course to us today, this sounds like an old legend or a nearly forgotten, moss-covered tale from yesteryear. But it is an actual tradition at that hermitage for who knows how long.

Keeping the place filled with supplies was a silent promise. It was a beautiful custom based on mutual dependence and human trust. There was nothing forced about it and there were no sanctions to be enforced if someone didn't keep the promise. It was done spontaneously, out of a spirit of free will and goodwill.

There's probably nothing more beautiful in this world than people relying on and trusting one another. Amidst a climate of mistrust, fear, and reluctance, even a contract signed on the finest and most durable paper in the world could never compare with a silent promise.

Awhile ago I spent a night at an isolated hermitage at an elevation of 1,700 meters. I couldn't rid myself of a lingering feeling of sadness when I saw that the built-in wall closet in such a small room had been locked. I tried to imagine what a closet at that elevation contained that could possibly be worth losing. Sadly enough, it appeared that at that hermitage there was no tradition of silent promises. *(1975)*

34. An Execution

"Are you really going to hang me now?"

We learned of these words spoken by a young man on death row from the newspapers. If I had just passed off the execution as society's way to seek retribution for a dastardly crime, there would be no problem; but for some reason the words continued to ring in my ears for days. In the early morning before the criminal was fully awake, he was chained and led into a strange room. He probably wasn't sure of what was happening until the executioner asked, "Do you have any last words?" He answered with his own question, "Are you really going to hang me now?" No doubt with tears of remorse falling onto his clothing, the twenty-two year-old then disappeared forever into the world of the gallows.

There's a saying that we should hate the sin but not the sinner. The day that I read the news of his execution, that young face of innocence, devoid of a single trace of bloodthirsty desire, kept flickering before my eyes. Of course, he's not the first person ever to be executed. But he became concrete proof to us of what had been little more than an abstraction before—the innumerable people who had gone before him onto the gallows.

When people live in a world in which for many it is so hard just to get by, they can at times lose their wits and harm others through temporary misjudgments or in the heat of the moment. And when people return to their senses, they tearfully look for a way to atone for what they have done. But today the law does not offer them the option to atone and start over. This is an age when "civilization" is supposed to have made great progress. Yet there is nothing more primitive than legal punishment: Those who kill have to be killed. If you look at these supposedly rational and ideal laws, the execution system is nothing more than murder as revenge.

Thoughts of revenge can be overcome only with loving-kindness. If people are not given the opportunity to atone for what they have done, they form a new grudge, and where can this grudge-bound spirit go? A grudge by society that results in the murder of a murderer can only breed another grudge in the murdered to look for another victim.

Astonishingly enough, there was an editorial cartoon that took aim at that execution in a very unexpected way: "Too bad they could only execute him once."

Such a statement stunned me. The criminal had only one body, so how many times did they want to kill him? This is precisely where we find anthropocentrism's blind spot. Love based on an anthropocentric view of the world inevitably results in confrontation and hate. The problem invariably becomes one of thinking only from an egotistical point of view.

Nowadays people go fishing or hunting in their leisure time. Those are, of course, forms of recreation and sport for the people involved, but they are a pressing matter of life and death for the fish and the wild animals. People consider fishing and hunting good use of their leisure time, but to creatures that stand to lose their one and only life, it is making bad use of their time. The inability to empathize with other forms of life is the blind spot of an anthropocentric approach.

There is no confrontation and hate in a thought system that respects all forms of life, since such people realize that we are all branches on the same tree. Genuine compassion is unconditional, absolutely impartial love. And only through such compassion can people become the real masters of all, including their own hearts.

"Are you really going to hang me now?"

This is not the language of a single condemned criminal. It is the cry of all forms of life that wish to live, the voice of the universe itself from deep within. *(1975)*

35. Temple Offerings

There's a lot of small talk nowadays in the Buddhist community about what exactly constitutes a temple offering. It originally meant something donated to a temple by a benefactor, but nowadays the term also includes things produced within the temple as well, since everything is a product of the four elements and therefore is, in a sense, an offering to us from the universe.

As a result, the temples are terribly severe even about a single grain of rice being washed away during the preparation of meals. Also, new aspirants working in a temple garden are often reprimanded about taking proper care of the crops and to do so as an offering. In a sense, this all seems to be overdone to the point of being parsimonious, but it is through such attention to detail that one develops proper practice. This is the very way in which Korean temples have been able to survive the upheavals of history for well over a thousand years.

Traditionally, monks meditate in a temple for three months and then take three months off to travel about seeking out teachers, doing volunteer service, or just helping out wherever their feet take them.

Once at the end of a meditation retreat, there were two young monks who had heard about a highly regarded scholar-monk, so they decided to seek him out. They had to walk a great distance through the summer heat and humidity to get to the monk's temple, and by the time they arrived they were exhausted. So they sat down to refresh themselves beside the stream that flowed by the temple. Suddenly one of them, with an expression of discouragement, suggested that they turn around and return to their temple. Taken aback, the other monk asked him why.

"Take a look at that!" he said as he pointed to a single leaf of lettuce floating down the stream. "What kind of teacher would live in a place that has so little regard for an offering? Let's go back to our temple."

"You're right about that. But, since we've come so far, the least we can do is just stop in the Buddha Hall and pay homage," said the other.

However, the first monk protested again. He insisted that they go back since there wouldn't be anything worth seeing in a temple that didn't have a real practitioner. Then suddenly, as they continued to argue back and forth, an old monk with a cane came teetering down to the stream, fished out the leaf of lettuce, and went back up to the temple.

Dumbfounded, the two young monks stared at each other for a moment, and then hustled their way up to the temple. They went into the guest quarters, put down their knapsacks, and went into the monk's room to give the elder monk proper greetings. They wound up studying under the monk for an extended period of time and made great progress in their practice.

*****

At lunar New Year's, usually in early or mid-February and several days before the end of the winter meditation season, there is a break from regular routines at temples and things are generally relaxed. So many monks climb up the snow-covered mountains and visit a hermitage or temple to give New Year's greetings to senior monks. Scholar-monks often spend the time in the temple lecture hall playing traditional holiday games.

Once, when I was living in a large monastery, a number of scholar-monks came into my room one night during the holiday period and turned the oil lamp way up so that we could better see the games as we played. The next morning, an older monk on his way back from duty at the temple office sent someone to tell me that he wanted to see me. I went to his room and he told me that because of our carelessness he suddenly had to resign his position. "When benefactors donate lamp oil to a temple, they expect monks to use it to study hard so that they can make progress and teach the people. Do you think that they donate it so that you can play games all-night long?"

From this, I learned a really good lesson in the true meaning of lay temple offerings and I dropped my head in shame.

Every now and then when I think about offerings made to the temple, the senior monk's words flash by like a streak of lightening. It's rather sad that nowadays it's hard to find such a wise old monk. *(1975)*

36. The True Light of Life

There are places always worth going to regardless of how life is treating you, and one of those places is the mountains. The mountains are beautifully wooded and the waters run clear. The birds and the beasts play exactly as they should, and cool breezes slide off the tree branches. The mountains are alive with bright sunshine, fresh forest fragrance, and primal mystique. These pristine forests offer nature as it is, without any artificial constraints on universal order. In addition, there are monasteries and monks scattered here and there. Put all of these things together and it's easy to see why people, tired and worn in both body and spirit, seek out the mountains whenever they can.

Recently, I spent about twenty days meandering around the mountains and valleys, and all the time I was conscious of the fact that the mountains were no longer what they used to be. They were falling apart, moaning under the strain of sadly ornamental park and tourism development projects. The stunning green pine forests and bamboo groves around the nation are becoming diseased and withered. Pine and bamboo are traditional symbols of purity and integrity. So we have to think about the meaning of their demise.

Even if tourism development secures much-needed foreign exchange, it is of more vital importance to protect our natural resources instead of letting them be desecrated mindlessly. For the most part, visitors to Korea do not come to see the latest industrial facilities or shimmering skyscrapers. They come because they have become wayfarers who are sick of the veneers of civilization and want to be held in the arms of unspoiled nature.

Yet even though the mountains are being ruined, it's fortunate that practicing monks are still able to live there. The mountains are the genuine Dharma halls for practice. They are living, thriving, harmonious ecosystems. And they are home to perfectly pure beings who exist like lotuses growing out of the muddy waters—such towering Korean Zen masters as Kyongbong, Songchol and Kusan, the true masters of the mountains.

Aside from these three great masters, there are plenty of young monks on mountains throughout the nation who sleep less every night in order to sharpen their knives. Not knives to harm other beings, but the knives of wisdom to cut through the deeply embedded roots of ignorance and delusion for themselves and for the people.

Every time I go to these Dharma Hall mountains, it's as warming as returning to my hometown for the first time in a long time. Just arriving washes away all the weariness of the trip to get there.

We don't go to these mountains because they are there. We go because they beckon us with their youthful vitality. We go because when spotless people and spotless environments harmonize, the two emit the true light of life. *(1975)*

37. "What More Could You Want?"

If you asked me when I feel best in my daily routines, I would unhesitatingly answer that it's right after shaving my head and bathing. Instinctively I feel clear and clean both inside and out, and that's when I feel most lighthearted. It feels like I've just been born.

The significance of shaving the head is the severing of secular attachments. Monastic regulations call for shaving the head and bathing twice a month, on the days before the new and full moons, respectively. But depending on the season and one's own considerations, it doesn't matter if monks do it more often. There are some Zen monks who do it everyday as part of their routine. The attempt to be totally spotless results in a very splendid, lighthearted feeling of innocence, and you feel like you're about to take off and soar like a bird. It's totally exhilarating.

About ten years ago I was staying at the Zen center of a major monastery. The large communal bathing facility for the monks was on the first floor. On one of the walls someone had written in candle wax, "What more could you want?" He had seemingly written it humorously after shaving his head and bathing, but it makes you wonder how exhilarated he must have felt if he had made the effort to write that on the wall. We're supposed to be greedless, but could there be anything greedier than this, than wanting the state where there's nothing left to be desired?

*****

There's an old adage that "a monk can't shave his own head." In a broader sense, it means that there are some things that even a professional can't do. For example, writers find it hard to proofread their own works so others have to do it for them. But concerning a monk not being able to shave his own head, nothing could be more further from the truth. In the temples monks shave each other's heads so everyone knows how to do it, even if they had never been a barber. Just about everyone can shave his own head. But how could you ever convey the feeling of satisfaction the first time you actually do it yourself?

A few years ago, the monk who had usually shaved my head for many years was hospitalized. I thought of asking another monk to do it for me, but I didn't want to impose so I decided to give it a try myself. To tell the truth, I had felt bad all those years bothering this or that monk to shave my head for me. And sometimes it occurred to me that I would have to do it if I ever were to go and live alone in an isolated hermitage.

I sat down and shaved very carefully, and contrary to expectations I did quite a fine job. I felt as good as if I were having my head shaved the very first time at initiation. And really, there was nothing more that I could have wanted in this whole world. Out of gratitude, I put on my robes and went up and paid homage to the Buddha.

I was so delighted that first time that, to commemorate the event, I went out the next day and bought a mirror and wrote on the back of it, "Shaved my own head" on such and such a date.

Ever since then, whenever I feel like it, I shave my own head in front of that mirror. It doesn't matter what kind of mood I'm in. Each time I do it, it's like being reborn. And sometimes if something's really bothering me, I'll shave my head again just to scrape and wash those cares away. *(1975)*

38. Renunciation

Strong winds started blowing through the forest yesterday, sounding much like waves rushing to shore along the coast. The forest trails will fill to the brim with fallen leaves. Once the leaves have all fallen and blanketed the ground, all that will be left will be the bare branches stretching up toward the early winter sky.

And what happens to the leaves? They get tossed about by the wind and finally come to rest under a tree or beside some plants where they lay down to rest and rot. Then in the spring, what's left is absorbed by the roots, travels up the sap, and transforms into new leaves or blossoms.

A personal transformation, too, is impossible unless you just leave, like the leaves that fall from their branches.

I returned to the mountains last autumn and the rustling of the fallen leaves woke me up several times during the night. The mountains don't talk, of course—at least in our language—but it was as if the rustling leaves out back were trying to wake me up. It seemed like the mountain winds were cleaning out my ears that had been clogged by the sounds of the secular world.

People have the determination to personally make changes in their surrounding environment, and that's true for organizations as well as for individuals. People in power strive to change their environment through the powers of their organizations. But the people who have no power and no organization find it difficult to change or restructure their environment. They know their limitations and they know that the best way to achieve their goals, without inconveniencing others around them, is to just drop it all and leave. They have to break out of the chains of a stifling situation and seek their own world.

Renouncing the world to become a monk is the same—leaving it all behind and just going. In Buddhism it's called "leaving home," since you're leaving the confinements, the attachments, and the conflicts of home life. It's also called "leaving greed," since you're leaving the fetters of greed that are inevitable in the secular world. And sometimes it's also called "leaving the dust," since you're leaving the world of dust and clutter, the world of mental dust and anguish. So renunciation is not a selfish attempt at escape but rather a positive search to discover eternal life.

*****

Monks are often asked why they left home to ordain. No doubt the inquirer is curious, but to us who are asked so frequently it sounds more like a broken record. Perhaps the inquirer is hoping to hear a juicy story that might be good enough for a scandal sheet, but since that's usually not the case, we feel bad at having to disappoint him.

Once when I was giving a Dharma talk, I said that if we had been brought up in the same environment as the Buddha Sakyamuni, we probably wouldn't have left home like he did. He had a beautiful wife, Yasodhara, and she was filled with inner wisdom and virtue. Both inside and out, she was a perfect soul mate for him.

As Siddhartha, before he became Buddha, he was also heir to the throne in an absolute monarchy. As king he would not be subject to the glares of the public, constitutional reforms, or impeachment procedures. And he would be set for the rest of his life as far as wealth was concerned. But he up and left all of that. Regardless of what anyone said he didn't want to live that way. Out of compassion for all beings, he longed to solve the riddle of suffering.

So why did I leave home and become a monk? Even if the Buddha were sitting right here, I would answer simply that I left to live as I should, to live the way I wanted to, to live the way that was best for me. I did not become a monk because of the impermanence of everything, nor because I was transfixed by the truth of Buddhism, nor because I was out to rescue sentient beings from suffering. In Buddhism we say that no one really has an anchor. We're all adrift on the sea of life. But secular life is not the only thing without an anchor. It's true for life as a monk as well, even though it may not appear that way.

I didn't really know much about Buddhism before I left home and came to the temple. And such lofty concepts as liberating sentient beings from suffering don't really apply to contemporary Korean Buddhism anyway. So of all the ways to live, why was it that I chose the path of a Buddhist practitioner, a disciple of the Buddha? It was hard to explain but it was something that my life demanded. And when the time is ripe, one cannot resist the tug of entwined karma accumulated over several lifetimes.

People are tremendously grateful, joyful, and content when they are able to live as they should, but when they can't, life is troublesome. People can't just waste this life away not fulfilling what they perceive as their role. That's when the practice of just dropping everything and leaving it all behind comes in handy. When one becomes lazy or powerless or when he feels that things just aren't right, he has to drop what he's doing and break out of the humdrum of his normal routines. Then, if he's still not satisfied, he has to just drop it and leave it all behind.

*****

In my twenty-odd years as a monk, I have become used to going through this type of karma, of dropping it all and leaving it all behind.

Trapped water stagnates. Water takes on a new life when it breaks out of a swamp and starts flowing towards the expansive ocean. Rolling, flowing water is so very much different from stagnating water.

An individual monk has a comparatively free lifestyle. In very early Buddhism, a monk was not even permitted to stay more than a day under a single tree. No doubt the concept of nonattachment was partially behind this, but probably more significant was the greater meaning of constantly moving, both to enhance practice and to teach. Later the tradition of spending the three-month rainy season in meditation wiped out the earlier tradition of constantly being on the move. But still these three-month retreats alternate with three months of moving about, when monks are free to flow and they're as unfettered as the drifting clouds and the flowing waters. This "drifting like the clouds and flowing like the waters" is undoubtedly the most lighthearted part of life as a monk.

The basic meaning of renunciation is not just shaving the head and practicing. Wearing different clothes and living a different lifestyle are merely superficial differences between monks and secular people. The real purpose of renunciation is to free oneself from artificial conditioning and to return to the original self. Otherwise renunciation has no meaning.

If people were completely content with their environment, then they would really not be very different from animals. But, as people, we're different. Through determined efforts, people reshape themselves and improve their environment as they go. This is what makes them capable of becoming higher sentient beings.

*****

You can't gain anything unless you rid yourself of something. And the great lesson of renunciation is that only those who give up a lot can gain a lot. By just dropping everything and leaving, one can continue to be reborn again and again—like the fallen leaves that return to the tree roots and reappear in the form of new buds.

The Buddhist terms no self or non-self do not eliminate the concept of self completely. They mean to eliminate the unnatural, superficial, egotistical, selfish self, to de-condition so that you can awaken to your true self. And it is traditional Indian thinking that this can be accomplished only by dropping everything, getting up, and leaving it all behind. Your determination to eliminate greed and desire has to be as great as the determination to actively seek the truth.

In one of his books Krishnamurti tells the story of a man who, with a towel on his shoulder, was about to go take a bath. His wife stopped him and started berating him: "You're hopeless. You're completely incompetent and as you get older all you do is eat and lay around. You couldn't live even a day without me. The man next door has a dozen or so concubines and he's getting rid of them one at a time. But you'd never even be able to do that."

The husband answered, "One at a time? Then he'll never be able to get rid of them all. If he were really going to get rid of them, he wouldn't do it one at a time. He'd do it all at once."

Not quite understanding what he meant, the woman continued to harangue him. Finally fed up, he said, "I'm the one who can really get rid of things, and not one by one. Just watch me. Here I go!" And he left the house just like that, with the towel on his shoulder. He had no intention of ever coming back, not even to get his personal belongings and tie up domestic affairs.

This is genuine "leaving greed" or "leaving home." Once you become fully aware of an unfavorable environment, you just get up and leave. All it takes is the determination to be able to break ties. If you try to rid yourself of one thing at time, it will take forever. But you can rid yourself of everything just by getting up and leaving it all behind. There may be some who feel that it would feel unnatural not to hold onto something, but only by leaving everything can you enjoy a truly lighthearted freedom: the freedom to live your own life. *(1976)*

39. Learning from the Forest

Having left the mountains and spent six or seven years in a temple near the big city, I gained a lot but I also lost quite a bit. What I gained was, through the firsthand experience of breathing in unison with these dizzying times, an appreciation of the realities of contemporary secular life. In the process, however, the pure light within me began to dim. For a practitioner on the path, this dimming of the inner light is not something to be taken casually. When a practitioner loses this light, his surroundings become as dark as he does.

The most disappointing thing to happen while I was at that urban temple was the gradual loss of the surrounding woods. I had relied on those flourishing woods for contemplation and movement, but they were felled for the ever-spreading city. And the rapidly increasing noise pollution was so bad that I could no longer hear my inner self. That is how the inner light began to fade.

A true practitioner belongs to the quiet and purity of the mountains. So last fall, after several years at the urban temple, I made arrangements and returned to the forest. I felt like a wild beast that had gone down to the fields, rummaged about, and finally returned exhausted to where I really belonged. Even though I did feel a heavy responsibility for having left my colleagues at the temple, I had no choice. I had begun to lose not only my inner light but my health as well.

The forest provides order and rest, quiet and peace. And in its generosity, it accepts everything that comes its way. It takes in the fog and the clouds, and the moonlight and the sunshine. It provides a home for birds and beasts. It refuses nothing, not even storms that ravish it. This magnanimity is the great virtue of the forest.

As soon as I returned to the forest, I could breathe once again. Handling the soil and seeing the trees cleansed me of the secular grime that had accumulated. With the clear wind blowing through me and the cool spring waters revitalizing both body and spirit, the garden of my heart began to sprout back to life. Winter passed, the vibrant colors of spring spread, the sap began to run. Once again I began to hear the basic sounds of nature that had been buried in the noise of the city. And once again, I furrowed and planted and weeded and nursed and finally ate the crops, and once again I was humbled anew by nature's magnificence.

Composed of earth and trees and water, nature knows not how to lie. It demonstrates to us the universal truth of reaping what you sow. In the face of such a principle, there can be no contrivance, trickery, or deceit. And there is absolutely nothing to correct or change in nature, since everything is complete and perfect. Everything that belongs there is there. If you look at everything honestly, then you get an honest response. All you have to do is have the patience to be tamed.

Last spring when fresh colors started to spread about the forest, I learned a great deal just by watching the harmony of nature. Each tree was beginning to display its own color, and not a single tree was being difficult or forcing its colors. With each tree just naturally exuding it own colors, the forest was achieving a dazzling harmony.

If all the trees were the same color, the forest would be dull and oppressive. It would be a soulless, gaunt forest rather than a nest of life. With their roots firmly implanted in the ground and their branches stretching into the air, the hearty trees strive to be themselves by sprouting their own colors. This is what makes the forest colors so dazzling and so harmonious. As we people drown in conformity and uniformity, we can't help but feel embarrassed in the face of such majestic harmony.

What does nature really mean to people?

Nature is much more than just a combination of earth and trees and water, more than just a huge ecosystem. And it is not something to be conquered. Do we as people, who cringe and creep about after a couple of hours of rain or a couple of centimeters of snow, have the right to talk about conquering something as mighty and majestic as nature? Instead, we should be humble enough to learn our own place and our limits directly from the order and magnanimity of the forest. The real human setting, rather than being the exhausting urban environment, is nature as it is. We have to repeatedly learn from nature how to live. We can find great meaning in the fact that humanity's great religions and thoughts emerged out of the forests and not out of classrooms. Nature is humanity's eternal mother.

But in this day and age we are destroying nature at an unprecedented rate. And what is more heartbreaking is that once destroyed, it can never be restored to its original state.

On weekends, go up to the mountains and look around the temples. There you'll be able to take a peek into the back yards of the nation. Every time I do, it strikes me that the quality of a nation does not depend just on export figures or per capital income. That quality should include how much a nation loves and cares for nature. *(1976)*

40. Walking Erect

I had some things to do today, so I went out into the world. The nearest city is about sixty kilometers from the hermitage, and as usual, it was bustling with people, noise, and dust when I arrived. I first went to the post office, and then I went to the market to buy some vegetables. I wound up buying a pair of fur-lined shoes as well. I also stopped off and bought some ointment for a small cut. I would have had to wait a long time for a bus back, so I took a different one headed in the same general direction, got off along the way, and walked back the remaining sixteen kilometers.

As I strode along the dikes of the freshly harvested fields and paddies, my head cleared from the bus ride and I felt reinvigorated. Walking is such a free, independent motion. It's such a delight to soak up the bright sunlight, to breathe in the invigorating air, and to saunter along flapping my wing-like arms. It's also great fun just to move along on my own, not dependent on anyone else for motion.

Sometimes when I really get into walking, I find myself whistling, and if the scenery is really nice, I can stop and cleanse my eyes by staring at the beauty. Walking with others can be fun, but walking by yourself is more relaxing than walking with someone you don't really get along with. Walking alone can also be a bit lonely, but that is the way of the wanderer.

Another good thing about walking is that you can also immerse yourself in thought if you like. You can take stock of the road you have traveled and the road before you.

We don't know when humans first began to think, but I suspect that it began when we began to walk. If you think a lot while remaining relatively stationary, your thoughts tend to go round in circles and you can become obsessed with something; but if you concentrate on something when you're walking, it's easier to go deeper and to solve a problem. I also think it's fair to say that Immanuel Kant, Ludwig von Beethoven, and other philosophers and artists derived a lot of their creativity from their strolls in the woods.

But it seems that now we are in the process of losing all of that, of losing ourselves. Since the invention of the automobile, we've had our walking gradually taken away from us. We're losing our ability to walk erect and to maintain a dignified posture. And in the process, we gradually began to forfeit our freedom of thought as well. Just take some crowded bus or train, and watch how your mind is taken over by others—by their bumping, shoving, and noise.

It makes me think of a line by a poet who said that for man, it was love at first sight with the automobile, so he married it; and that he'll never ever return to a pastoral way of life.

Walking back those sixteen kilometers, I felt like this tiny body in a gigantic universe had found a place to rely on, although I was just passing through. I also felt that these precious paths were, for bugs as well as for beasts, places for them to rely on as they diligently go about their daily lives.

I feel both grateful and lucky today that I had the chance to walk so far. For the first time in a long time, instead of taking the bus to the city and back, I was walking my own way, moving on my own feet, walking erect. *(1977)*

41. "Have A Cup of Tea!"

Life in the mountains during the winter consists largely of heating, cooking, eating, and meditating. About the time a frigid high-pressure area centered over Mongolia was tenaciously taking hold, I had a particularly difficult time. When living alone in a hermitage, a monk has to try to come to terms with laziness, a trap that is easy for many people to fall into when they lead an independent life. Boredom can be another problem, particularly on days like today when it's snowing. I thought I'd remain indoors all day not doing much of anything.

I yawned at the snow. But then I looked out at the forests and peaks. They seemed as if they had been brushed over with a very pale wash of India ink. Suddenly I found myself sliding out the door into the woods.

Like a wild beast, I roamed about here and there in the valleys until my tattered clothes and fur hat became soaked from snow and sweat. With the untimely appearance of a human, roe deer sprang away, pheasants flew off in a fuss, and wild rabbits rustled around in the bamboo groves. I worried about what they all had to eat in this cold, a cold that had frozen the skies as well as the earth.

I came back to the hermitage and lit an armful of firewood. As I sat in front of the fire, its swirling flames dried my clothes. When you look at the flames of a good fire, something lights up inside as well. I suddenly had the urge to make something, so I dug out the saw and other tools from the toolbox and went to work. Echoes of my efforts resonated throughout the valley. The wind howled and the snow blowing off the top of the bamboo groves created a blizzard of its own. The bamboo, which had been weighed down by the snow, sprang back up and danced in the wind.

I fetched some water from the spring and made a pot of tea. I could hear the forest winds echo even in the brazier. Didn't they say that one forgets the cares of the world when having a cup of tea? The delicate taste is indescribable.

Someone once wrote, "As I become absorbed in drinking a few cups of tea by a bamboo grove, a strange fragrance filters into the hand holding the cup." In other words, everything seems to become one. The virtue of having tea every now and then is that it helps to keep daily life in the mountains clear and lucid.

And someone else wrote, "When drinking tea, if there are too many guests it becomes noisy, and if it's noisy, the air of refinement disappears. It's refreshing and refined if you drink alone, and nice and quiet when two drink together. It's fun if three or four drink together; kind of flat if five or six drink together; and if seven or eight drink together, everything gets lost in the process of pouring tea for so many." Indeed, the air of refinement begins to disappear as the number of participants increase.

The renowned Ch'an Master Chaochou offered tea to everyone who came to see him. One day, two scholar-monks who had come to study under him came to his room to give him greetings. Master Chaochou asked one monk if he had come to his room before, to which he replied, "No, this is my first time."Master Chaochou followed up with, "Is that so? Then have a cup of tea!"And he poured him a cup.

Master Chaochou then asked the other monk if he had come to the room before and he answered that he had. Master Chaochou said,

"Well then, have a cup of tea!"

Later, the housekeeper, who had watched this and had thought it strange, asked Master Chaochou, "Excuse me Master, but how is it that you gave a cup of tea to both the monk who had been here before and the monk who hadn't?"

Master Chaochou stared at him and hollered, "Housekeeper!"

Startled, the housekeeper answered meekly with a "Yes?"

"Have a cup of tea!"

I wonder what Master Chaochou's tea tasted like. If we knew, we would have also tasted Master Chaochou's meaning at the same time. When you have a cup of tea, you are drinking everything around you.

They say that in the days when Zen was a way of life, the Way of Tea, filled with color and fragrance and taste, flourished. But nowadays, tea tastes pretty much the same wherever you go. And that's because Zen is the exclusive property of monks who keep it confined to the meditation centers.

Even so, whatever you're doing now, please stop and just have a cup of tea! *(1977)*

42. Zen and the Art of Robbery

Once there was an old robber. When he felt his inevitable death coming nearer and nearer, he decided that he couldn't leave this world without passing on his lifelong skills and secrets of success. He wanted to pass on this accumulated expertise to at least one person, even if it were his own son.

So one night the robber took his son along on his chores to "get a feel for the night dew." Nowadays, thieves probably set their schedules around the most popular television programs when people are intently distracted, but in the old days they inevitably worked in the pitch black of a moonless night. And in the old days there were no really luxurious homes, so the most popular choices for robbers were homes without watchdogs, regardless of the height of the wall to be scaled.

So father and son first chose a house. Then they nimbly made their way over the wall and headed straight for the storeroom in which sat a very large rice chest. The father opened the chest and pushed his son into it. Then suddenly he shut the door and locked the chest with the nearby padlock. He then ran out of the storeroom and as he leaped back over the wall, he started screaming "Thief! Thief!"

Startled, the family tore through the house looking for a thief. The robber's son himself was no less stunned than the family members. Feeling his father had betrayed him, he was at a loss at what to do. But then he became so completely outraged at this father that he swore to get out of this predicament and tell his father off.

Stuck in the rice chest, he finally started squealing like a rat. The owner opened the storeroom door and glanced around but didn't see a thing. The robber's son let out another squeal. This led the owner over to the rice chest and he carefully unlocked it. As soon as he did, the robber's son leaped out of the chest, then out the storeroom door, back over the wall and down the path. There was a well on the path up ahead and as the son ran by it in the dark, he plopped a large boulder into it. Those in hot pursuit heard the splash and figured that the thief must have fallen into the well and drowned, so they returned home.

The son arrived at his home out of breath. He became even more indignant at seeing his father sitting there completely calm. He was about to confront him when the father, with a broad grin of satisfaction on his face, said, "You escaped the trap I set for you! You're worthy of carrying on my trade!"

And this is the way the father had taught his son, without a single word, the tricks of the trade. He taught by providing experience rather than words so that the son could figure out the secrets himself.

The story comes from the Chinese Sung dynasty Master Fayan who was trying to explain Zen. The point is that Zen is not something you learn from outside, from education, or from theory; rather, it's something that you have to experience. And it's not something to be understood from an objective point of view; it's something that has to be intuitively grasped. It's the process of awakening to your limitless inner potential through complete immersion. That is why they say

Zen is based on experience rather than knowledge. Zen becomes a living thing when this unlimited creativity expresses itself to others through the warmth of compassion and the light of wisdom.

When Zen is something that lives only in a meditation center, it is no different than being caught in a rice chest. It becomes a creative function only when it leaps out of the chest and makes its way into the world of people. *(1977)*

43. A Good Day Every Day

Life seems to be just a series of repetitions. We get up, have three meals, and go to bed. People go to work and come back at conventional, regulated times. Sometimes we love, sometimes we hate, sometimes we have regrets, and sometimes we make new resolutions. But for the most part, we just flounder around in the swamp of the same daily habits amidst the beginningless and endless flow of things.

If this were our entire life, we'd probably just give up and turn in the remaining time that we had. But if we look closely, we can see that no two days are exactly the same. I'm not the same person today that I was yesterday and tomorrow I won't be the same person I am today. Fortunately, we're not pieces of furniture that just sit around; nor are we the hands of a clock that go around in circles. Life is a constant process of transformation and it can become as dynamic as a person wants it to be.

A Zen master once told his disciples, "I won't ask you what you've been doing. But I want each of you to tell me what you're going to do." His message of course was to forget about the past and to think about the future. Not a single disciple responded. Before long, the master had to provide an answer: "Every day is a good day."

Contrary to popular belief, this old Zen saying doesn't mean that every day is a good day regardless of what happens. Striving with complete awareness and determination, we should continually be reborn in each and every new moment every day. And then every day becomes a good day.

People who flounder around in the same old habits every day lose control of their lives. But those who are constantly aware of what their lives are all about have control.

What is the meaning of the fact that no two people have the same faces and the same voices? We are all wanderers who have been invited to take part in the harmonization of the universe through our distinct personalities and capabilities. We don't need clones of Jesus or Buddha. Rather, we need people who can make the most of their own personalities and capabilities. Through such a process, each one of us becomes a new contribution to the world. Those who disregard their uniqueness and capabilities and who live with one-track minds are no more than revisionists who are doing human history a disservice.

There are people all around us who suffer one way or another everyday, so how could every day be a good day for them? But it is through that daily suffering that we can find meaning in life. Our lives carry with them the responsibility of meeting challenges with determination so as to overcome our sufferings. We have to take each day as a new opportunity for growth so that we can discover the true meaning of our lives that are filled with contradictions and conflicts. We weren't meant to live our lives just like everyone else; we have to make the most of our own lot. We can make every day a good day for ourselves and for others by finding deeper meaning in our daily lives. *(1977)*

44. Kitchen Motto

There's plenty to do at a hermitage as fall fades into winter. And having to do everything by myself at an isolated hermitage like this in the mountains, I find my arms and legs are going all the time. For starters, I have to ready a winter's worth of firewood, give the Buddha Hall a good cleaning, and get a winter's supply of kimchi ready. I can now really get a feel for the old saying that "a monk in the fall needs nine feet."

It's tiring, but it's worth it since I can live the way I wish. Of course, if you are living in a group as they do in the larger temples, all of these chores get done much more easily through group effort. But I no longer wish to live that way. I felt that it really wasn't contributing to my progress on the Path.

Since becoming a monk, I have lived in many large temples, and particularly over the last few years I've seen a lot and heard a lot. In the process it seems that I was starting to become somewhat of a grouch. Of course, we can find meaning by living in a group and thereby learning to rely on one another and to live in harmony with others. But I hated the complaining. On top of that, the traditional monk's way of life is fading fast. I had renounced the secular life and became a monk all by myself, and now I've left the big temples to live as a solitary monk. The life of a true monk is as solitary and one-pointed as the horn of a rhino.

Living like this is no easy task. There are plenty of times when cooking for yourself can be more irritating than enjoyable. But since eating is essential to health, you have to do it. And you have to eat it all or it spoils and goes to waste. But no one living alone goes to great lengths to cook up a storm. If I really wanted to eat well, all I'd have to do is go live in a temple in a high-flying urban setting.

When I came to this place in the mountains, the first thing I did was make a table. If I were to eat in the small room, I'd have to make several trips back and forth to the kitchen and if I were to eat in the kitchen I'd need a table. So I got some old boards and put them together for a table and made a chair out of black oak logs. Sitting at the table reminded me of the movie Papillon, so I called the table the "Papillion table."Papillon confirmed his own existence though his unbridled determination to escape the injustices and pressures of prison life.

On my Papillon table I wrote the words "simple and plain." That became the kitchen motto for my hermitage. Of course the life of a mountain monk should be simple and plain all around, but I wrote this anyway to remind me each time I ate to keep eating simply. I find that if I have too many things on a table, my mind scatters and everything loses its taste.

My friends worry about my health when they see my simple and plain meals, but it has been my experience that food isn't the only factor that contributes to good health. I spent a winter on another mountain once, subsisting on nothing but salt and soy sauce, and having that only once a day. A monastic monk is not a monastic monk if he eats everything he wants and sleeps whenever he wants. We should just be grateful, as well as even a bit embarrassed, by a meal.

On really cold days, I don't look forward to going into the kitchen. Knowing my idiosyncrasies, a colleague at one of the larger temples offered to send up a temple cook to prepare my meals. But for the first time in a long time, I took the liberty of refusing a kind gesture. I like simple, plain food and a simple, plain life. I like the lighthearted feeling that goes with it. *(1977)*

45. The Boundless Sea

Having lived in the mountains for a long time, sometimes I suddenly get homesick for the sea. In the mountains, with the ridgelines obstructing the view, I begin to miss the great expansiveness that the sea provides. Last winter, upon receiving a postcard sent from the East Coast, I was filled with a strong sudden urge to seek out the ocean again. Had it not been meditation season, I probably would have gone right then and there.

Whenever I enjoy a bowl of chilled seaweed strips, I can practically hear the waves crashing on the shore and the cries of the seagulls. And I can feel the refreshing salty sea breezes all over my body. I could hardly wait for the meditation season to end so that I could take off on the first bus the very next day. Which is exactly what I did.

The nearest seaside, the renowned Hallyeosudo Waterway along the southern coast, was about 125 kilometers away. The spring sea there is so tranquil and beautiful. The handsome islands and pretty islets appear to be dozing on the placid waters, and the scattered fishing boats move as leisurely as the waterway birds. The stunning serenity is like a scene from another world. There, at that time of year, the sea is more like a huge placid lake.

It had been some time since I had seen the sea, so I boarded a ferry for a trip through the waterway. But I was not about to put up with the claustrophobia of the passenger cabin. I remained on the deck where

I was able to free my eyes from confinement like that which had been imposed on me by the mountain ridges. As the boat glided through the waters, I quickly ventilated my fermented forest lungs with plenty of salty sea breezes.

The ocean accepts waters from all rivers, and, in the process, the rivers lose their identity once they flow into the ocean. All the waters become one in the waves of eternal life. And there's nothing that the ocean won't accept—it takes everything in as its own, even pollution. Thus it is considered the mother of redemption.

There are places along the coast that offer a wonderfully unobstructed view of the vast ocean. And whenever I encounter the boundless sea, my niggling daily routines disappear completely. I can see primal nature on the endless horizon and I become conscious of myself as part of that infinity. My usually structured, strict life becomes, right there and right then, as unfettered as a sea breeze, and as I free myself of fixed ideas and preconceptions, new horizons open up for me.

The cities where people have converged to make their living are dying day by day. But the sea is forever alive with waves of motion. And it is this sea that revives and revitalizes all of us scarred and worn down by urban existence so that we may have brighter and happier tomorrows. *(1977)*

46. Mosquito Talk

The weather had been getting hotter and the meditation room stuffier. So a few days ago I began leaving the front and back doors open for ventilation. I can also hear the languid calls of the cuckoo riding in on the faint fragrance of the forest. Occasionally, a butterfly will drift in or a bumblebee will come in to bob about and bounce off the walls and ceiling. Once in a while even a lost bird will fly in but then suddenly flap its way out upon seeing the offerings on the altar. These are all members of the mountain family and we all live together.

However, today I unintentionally committed murder. A short while ago while I was meditating, a bumblebee came in and started bouncing about and buzzing back and forth right in front of my eyes. Aggravated, I shouted "Get out, you little #%$*!" and then tried to swish him away with the wooden clapper. But, inadvertently, I hit him and he fell dead to the floor. I was out of sorts for the rest of the day. How pitiful. The bee had come into this world, to this mountain to live, and then to this room to play, only to get clobbered by a monk and die.

Some might think it weird that I'd get so upset over the death of an insect, particularly at a time when in the current state of world affairs human life seems to have become less valuable than even the life of a fly. But that type of thinking is highly anthropocentric. From a bug's viewpoint, it's still regrettable to lose its only life so senselessly.

As a result of their own karma, people and animals look different, but there is not an iota of difference in their will to live. And there is no rule that the weak have to be killed for the stronger. Think how you'd feel if, for example, a huge bear carried off your cute little kids for a meal.

Human lives cannot be a means to an end for others; they are perfect ends in themselves. And that is the sole, absolute value. Therefore, there can be no excuse for injuring or tormenting a form of life that wants to live. That is an incomparable evil. All forms of life, even microbes, are interdependent. And it is the interaction of everything that provides the harmony, balance, and order of the universe.

In the old days monks used to make their straw sandals as soft and loosely knit as possible, rather than tightly bound and firm, so as not to crush bugs and insects along the mountain trails. In the summer meditation season, there still is a basic intention in practice not to step on a single bug when walking around. Compassion is not limited solely to people; it's love and caring for all forms of life. This belief in the absolute nature of all forms of life is traditional Oriental thought.

Last summer I heard a story about mosquitoes from an old monk, and, even though it's a parable, I was struck silent by its simple message.

Around dusk one night, a mother-in-law mosquito was getting ready to go out and she said to her daughter-in-law mosquito, "Don't bother getting supper ready for me." Thinking this strange, the daughter-in-law mosquito asked why not.

Gazing out at a mountain, the mother-in-law mosquito replied rather mournfully, "If I'm lucky enough to run into a nice person tonight, I'll be able to eat well by myself. But if I run into someone cruel, I'll be killed. So either way, there's no need to get my supper ready."

Whenever I hear a mosquito buzzing around me, I instinctively raise my hand to swat it, but then I immediately think of the mother-in-law mosquito, and I lower my hand. Even if I haven't become nice, at least I don't want to become cruel. *(1977)*

47. Dharma Home

There are times when a person really doesn't know what to do with their life, so he or she leaves home to become a monk.[1] There are two ways of doing this. The first is to just show up at the temple where they may find, as a new novice, a teacher; or they may be assigned a teacher later after taking final ordination. The second way is to find a teacher in advance, become a disciple, and then join the temple as a novice under this teacher. The latter is more desirable since as a novice the aspirant will receive traditional training and guidance from his teacher.

Whichever the case, the temple where the aspirant goes for initiation and ordination serves as a psychological cradle for the monks for the rest of their lives. Memories of novice life follow a monk around like a shadow wherever they go and whatever they do. There are times when I become so nostalgic that I wish I could return to that early novice life.

My Dharma home, the temple where I first had my head shaved as I renounced the secular world, was on an island in Chungmu (now Tongyang) on the southeast coast. It was really more like a hermitage than a temple, having only three buildings including the outhouse. There's a bridge to the island now, but at the time we had to walk through a tunnel under the waterway to get to it.

Behind the temple, a peak shot up into the air out of a wall of rock, and the temple was surrounded by pristine cypresses. Usually we could look out to the ocean with its expansive horizon, but during the summer

[1] In the Korean Mahayana tradition, both males and females may take full ordination. Korea, in fact, has the world's only female order of monks, the Bomun Order. However, most take ordination with the Jogye Order.

monsoons, the fog was so thick we could hardly see anything and we had to keep bailing out the fuel holes in order to light fires for cooking.

It was not long after the end of the Korean War when I joined the temple. Even now I can vividly recall having my share of hardships, including being constantly hungry. It was a Zen meditation temple and discipline was harsh. For breakfast we had a bowl of thin porridge and for supper we had a spoonful of rice left over from lunch. Nothing in this world has ever tasted as good as a few noodles that tried to escape while I was rinsing them at the well one day.

In addition to the hunger, I had my share of nosebleeds from the strain of labor that I wasn't used to, and I still have vivid memories of literally crawling back from the outhouse on all fours on more than one occasion after severe intestinal outpourings left me totally drained.

In the early days, I was "the wood bearer" in charge of the wood. Three times a day I had to go fetch wood, chop it up, and light the fires in the fuel holes. During my early years, I was able to complete the more burdensome tasks thanks largely to the strength I derived from my teacher, Master Hyobong, and his Dharma lessons. Even so, in comparison to the trials and tribulations of monks in the old days, my own hardships were embarrassingly negligible.

Even now, decades later, still the best way for me to combat the tendency to kick back and take it easy when meditation season ends is to head for my Dharma home. By returning there I can relive the eagerness, enthusiasm and naiveté of novice life and reflect on my current life as well.

*****

My Dharma home temple is quite different now. New buildings have replaced the old ones and the doors are high enough that I don't bang my head on the transoms. There's electricity, so we no longer have to worry about candles starting fires. There's good food and everything is quite convenient, but it's a bit sad to see that there are so few practitioners now.

In my early days, there were about twenty novices and monks going back and forth and calling the place home. Last spring, as I walked along the wooded paths around the temple, I counted those of us who were still around from that time twenty years ago, and there were only four. About half of those gone had passed away and the other half had de-robed at one time or other to return to secular life.

Of the monks who had passed on, one died not so long ago. He had immersed himself totally in meditation as a hermit in an isolated cave on the mainland for fifteen years. In order not to impose on anyone, he picked his own bracken and survived on whatever else he found. His only possession was the set of ragged robes that he was wearing when he passed on. He knew the time was coming and he sat in the lotus position until the very end. That is how they found him. *(1977)*

48. Vehicle for Offerings

In the old days monks frequently said that there was nothing more difficult than life as a monk. I often heard them say, "It's really a tough way to get three meals a day."And whenever I heard that, I thought the monks were saying it out of humility. But nowadays, what they said suddenly comes to mind quite often and I can easily empathize with them. At first glance it might seem that there's nothing easier and more comfortable than life as a monk. Upon closer observation, however, one can see that there probably is no work more difficult.

A monk's life does in fact probably look like it's a much easier way to get three regular meals a day than, say, it is for a low-wage blue-collar worker who toils under the blazing sun. And it probably is in fact more comfortable than the life of someone who breaks his back trying to keep his dependents clothed and fed, and provide his children with a decent education like everyone else. But think about it: Would anything be more corrupt and unfair than some people leisurely sitting around waiting for it all to come in while others lived rather tragic existences just trying to make a living?

In this world of ours, there's no such thing as a free lunch. It would go against the very basic nature of everything. The undeniable law of the universe is that you reap what you sow. This law of cause-and-effect guarantees that if you work up a debt in any form, you'll have to pay for it sooner or later, one way or another. And that's what makes monks not only wary but even frightened of offerings to the temple.

People don't always bring offerings to the temple out of the pure goodness of their hearts when they have surpluses at home. They are so busy with their secular lives that they don't have the time to do proper Buddhist practice, so they make offerings at a temple in hopes that the monks will do it for them in return for the offerings. They are asking us to practice for them since they can't renounce the secular world, join a monastery, and practice properly themselves.

So, contrary to popular opinion, it's neither biological demands nor complicated interpersonal relationships that make the life of a monk so difficult. Nor is it due to the demands of national campaigns or of a monk's particular sect. What makes life so difficult for us is the fact that we have to serve as a medium to earn merit for others. We have a tough enough time trying to get our own hearts in order and yet we're expected to be a medium for others as well.

Another thing that makes life difficult for a monk is that we are expected to function as the Sangha itself. This means that we serve as a refuge for others. When people who could be my parents or grandparents come to me, prostrate, and take refuge in the Sangha, I have to think about whether or not I really deserve to serve as a refuge for them. That's a frightening responsibility. Because of this formidable responsibility, I can't really accept or reject their refuge, and that's what's so hard.

A monk's work doesn't end by becoming awakened through sutra study or enlightened by solving a koan. Those are merely means to an end rather than ends in themselves. Such things wouldn't be Buddhism or even religion if they were ends in themselves. That is what happened when Indian Buddhism mixed with Chinese Taoism—the means became confused with the ends.

The duty of a monk is to liberate the infinite number of sentient beings from the seas of darkness and ignorance, and from the swamps of absurdity and unreasonableness. If we turn our backs on these responsibilities, if we no longer serve as a medium for people and as the Sangha refuge, then we can't avoid being castigated as nothing but lazy freeloaders. So let's stop for a moment and really ask ourselves what we are doing for today's society. *(1977)*

Part III:

The Sound of Water, The Sound of Wind

49. Endless Renunciations

The other day in the middle of a downpour, a young fellow in his twenties arrived at the main temple soaking wet. Having already had the experience of renunciation myself, as soon as I saw him I could tell by his tense expression and silence why he had come.

He had probably spent several sleepless nights going through a Hamlet-type of conflict and finally took the decisive measure of leaving home for good. Although a broad variety of different circumstances lead people to make that choice, the tormenting decision to snap off the branch of family life is undoubtedly the same for everyone. Each has stood before those earnest and urgent questions—"Who am I?""What am I living for?""How should I be living?"—leaving them no choice but to make a drastic change in the course of their lives.

In the face of such basic questions, a young person's lucid sensitivities can't help but become afflicted. Since they are human and can think for themselves, they are not yet ready to cast themselves into a gray world filled with complacency and routines and conventions. At that age, they want to be reborn again and again and to redefine their lives so that they can continue to grow.

This incident reminded me of the time when I renounced the world myself. I was about the same age. I thought I was the only one in the world going through the torment of wrestling with the meaning of life. I stayed up wide-awake night after night getting no answers to my questions. Then the Korean War broke out and everything became confusion. Order and values went out the window. Survival was not the top priority; it was the only priority.

At the time, several friends thought that crossing the sea to Japan would lead to a bright new life and were excited about becoming stowaways. The rest of us were poor students, but we still emptied our nearly empty pockets to give them farewell parties. Another friend could not cope with the torments of existence and turned in the rest of his life, so to speak. Everyone else seemed to have their wits about them, so why was it that my friends and I had to go through such torments? Now that I think about it, we were afflicted with an unusually severe case of growing up and the war had exacerbated it.

Once I had made up my mind to renounce the world and join a temple, I was able to shed all of my inner struggles and conflicts. It wasn't until later that I was really able to understand how I had felt. Renunciation had been like diving into the middle of the ocean—not to drown myself but, armed with the will to live, to search and search to the very depths of life.

So that is why they say that renunciation, rather than being a negative escape from secular life, is a positive commitment to search for life's meaning. It's up to each of us to try to rely solely on our own and to live our lives to the utmost, since no one else can do it for us. The act of leaving home can either be called "renunciation"or "running away," depending on whether you are searching for something or escaping from something.

What had held me back was my collection of books. My family was not well-off, but as an only son I had a comparatively free and carefree life, thanks largely to the loving care of my grandmother for her only grandson. If I were to renounce everything and go to the temple, I would have to renounce that collection of books, my only possessions, which I had treasured for years. For three or four nights in a row, I'd take out a few of the books that I loved most and wanted to keep, then reconsider, and then put them back. I did this over and over. It was a terrible attachment. If I were feeling that way just over a few books, I wondered how people felt who were leaving a wife and kids. That was worth thinking about. Finally, I decided on three books, wrapped them up, and brought them along with me when I went to the temple. Later, everyone else thought that those books were boring and of no help whatsoever.

Renunciation isn't just a question of physically appearing at the temple. You have to be able to come to the temple having forsaken all of your attachments and contradictions, and conflicts and habits, because in order to gain a lot, you have to give up a lot. That is why we sometimes call renunciation "the huge dumping"—you literally and psychologically have to dump everything. You have to become free of all of your possessions, your conditioned ideas, your habits, and your artificialities in order to become totally free. Being totally free means having the ability to totally control your tri-karma of thinking, speaking and doing.

That is why the initial renunciation is not the last. You have to keep on renouncing over and over. Monks are sentient beings, and as such, they, too, have their share of worldly contradictions and conflicts. And these external conflicts are not the only things you have to renounce. You have to continue to renounce the endless number of inner conflicts as well. So renunciation is an endless series of extrications; and monastic life is like an endless track of hurdles to leap.

I wonder about the young fellow who came to the temple a couple of days ago. Tomorrow I should go down to the temple to see how he's getting along and handling his conflicts. *(1978)*

50. Buddhist Views on Good and Evil

Even from the earliest sutras, Buddhism taught that the basic nature of humanity is pure and spotless. The Buddha said, "This heart of ours is originally pure; but the heart becomes soiled from time to time by one's karma."

In other words, as things happen to us throughout our lives, how we behave and react determine how soiled our hearts become. There is no such concept as "original sin" in Buddhism, so rather than repenting over sins or misdeeds, we search for ways to cleanse our hearts of the Three Poisons of avarice, aversion, and ignorance (of truth), so that we can return to the natural condition of purity.

In doing so, we first have to turn to the issue of what constitutes good and evil.

"Good" and "evil" are easy to define theoretically but the dichotomy becomes rather hazy in our daily lives. A single action can seem good from one perspective and evil from another. We've all experienced enough of these situations in our own everyday lives.

Buddhism's definition of "good"and "evil"can also be a bit vague at times, but generally in Buddhism, "good" is anything that benefits beings, while "evil" is anything that harms them, anything that causes suffering. Some sutras emphasize that you have to determine what is just and what is not, and that which is just is good. In this case, we use the Pali word "attha,"which means profit, so something that profits others is good and it is just. Buddhist Dharma is good, since it is just. From the Sutta Nipata we have:

> It's easy to identify the wealthy
> And it's easy to know ruin.
> Those who love the Dharma are rich
> And those who ignore the Dharma come to ruin.
>
> If you consort with evildoers
> And distance yourself from the gentle,
> And if you like what the evildoers do,
> Then you invite your own ruin.

Evil refers to unfavorable and harmful action, and this includes the breaking of any community rules. Generally, in religious circles, this means breaking the precepts, commandments or other regulations.

But in Buddhism, evil is a different issue. It is often even called "non-good" rather than "evil." Buddhism is more concerned with where this behavior comes from rather than with the behavior itself. And it is more concerned with eliminating the causes of such behavior than with punishing the behavior.

There is a very famous quote from both the early Theravada and the Mahayana sutras:

> Do no evil.
> Do only good.
> Cleanse the mind.
> This is the teaching of all the buddhas.

The importance of cleansing the mind is the teaching of all those who have become enlightened, and thus this has become an important lesson that Buddhism emphasizes over and over. One must turn inward and cleanse the heart. All the atrocities of society arise from hearts that have not been cleansed of anguish. It is precisely these anguishes resulting from the Three Poisons that give rise to social troubles and evil. And since we are all the building blocks of society, it is the anguish within each of us that invariably and inevitably spreads beyond us to society in general.

Anguish Leads to Evil

In Buddhism we often refer to the 108 or the 84,000 anguishes or torments. The numbers in themselves have no particular significance since in the ancient Indian tradition they just meant "many"or "innumerable." Of these innumerable anguishes, the Three Poisons are the most pernicious. Many sutras expounded upon these as the roots of all non-good. In Buddhist practices these Three Poisons have to be avoided and conquered. The Three Poisons are often referred to as the "Three Fires."

The first of these, avarice (including greed, desire, and coveting) becomes the source of unreasonable desires to possess. It also leads to fixations. The greed to take or have what belongs to others is considered an evil. Another form of this is the thirst for more and more, which is often based on envy and greed for what belongs to others. Consequently people can never become satiated, no matter how much they accumulate. Enough never seems to be enough. The proliferation of materialism has cast us into an age when the thirst for more and the desire to possess more have enslaved us all. And this overextended personal greed is by its very nature evil because of what it results in.

Aversion in any form, including anger and hate, is the second of the Three Poisons. It is considered evil because it has negative effects on others. Like greed, anger and hate are directed at what is outside of us. We become greedy for that which we love and become angry with that which we hate. Both of these cause problems not only for us but for others as well.

The third poison, ignorance, or foolish thinking, is another source of non-good or evil behavior. In Buddhism ignorance is the failure to see the true reality of nature, and this results in foolish behavior. It is living without the wisdom that is inherent within all of us.

These poisons, summed up as ignorance and craving, are not, however, inherent. Buddhism teaches us that our basic nature is good. It is as pure and shiny as gold. So eliminating ignorance and craving can lead to enlightenment. Basic Buddhism teaches that evil can be stopped by good, and that by doing good, we can eliminate ignorance and folly. This sets the foundation for morality in Buddhism.

Uprooting Evil

Let's take a look at how to uproot evil. Buddhism is distinguished from other religions of the Indian subcontinent in many ways, and one way is that it teaches the concept of the interdependence of everything. Following the laws of interdependence, nothing exists on its own. Early on the Buddha taught, "Since there is this, there is that. Since this does not exist, that does not exist."

This applies to individuals as well as to objects. As a member of society, each person is in innumerable ways intrinsically intertwined with the rest of society. Even though we always talk about "I" and "my", those are inaccurate terms based on conditioning. To perceive life from such a vantage is, in Buddhist terms, ignorance. Such ignorance results in hatred and greed and the tainting of our originally pure nature. The best way to understand all of this is to impartially observe the true nature of everything.

Thus goodness is being free from the Three Poisons of avarice, aversion and ignorance of truth. Even the early sutras point to this. The following is a bit repetitive, but it makes the point:

"Ignorance is the root of all evil. Ignorant of this ignorance, an unwise person will develop wicked tendencies, and such a slant will give rise to wicked thoughts. Wicked thoughts then give rise to wicked language, which in turn gives rise to wicked behavior. This in turn leads to a wicked life. And a person who leads a wicked life makes wicked efforts, which in turn lead to a wicked mind. A person with a wicked mind will concentrate on wicked things."

This quote from a sutra points out the interrelatedness of ignorance to wickedness, which can arise in various forms. On the other hand, the sutras talk about the role of wisdom in the gradual path to enlightenment. Wisdom, the opposite of ignorance, leads to goodness in attitude, thought, language, behavior, effort, mind, memory and concentration.

In order to rid oneself of the Three Poisons, we should rely on the Three Baskets (a.k.a. Three Studies) of Buddhism—Discipline, Meditation, and Wisdom. Avarice can be overcome by knowing who you are and by relying on the pure standards of the Precepts. Aversion can be overcome through the pure concentration of meditation. And ignorance can be overcome by wisdom.

Buddhist Training Precepts

The codes of behavior for a Buddhist way of life include refraining from the Three Poisons as well as practicing the Five Lay Precepts. These are training precepts or guides along the path of morality that will lead to eventual awakening through proper behavior. The Five Precepts date from the time of the Buddha and they have been passed down to us through Mahayana Buddhism for the laity. These precepts are refraining from taking life in any form; from taking what does not belong to you; from verbal misconduct; from adultery; and from using mind-altering substances like alcohol and drugs.

At first, people may misinterpret these as being commandments of "don't do this"or "don't do that"; but they are in fact voluntary codes of training that have the meaning of "I will refrain" from this or that because of the unfavorable consequences that may result.

The first, to refrain from taking life, is not restricted to human life. It refers to all forms of life, as an expression of the Buddhist concern and compassion for everything living. It is a religious ethic based on respect for all forms of life. In Buddhism killing or harming anything that has the will to live is considered evil, and it transcends categories and ideologies. One must not kill directly, order others to kill, watch such killing, or even tolerate it. In addition, all forms of life are afraid of violence, so we should also put an end to violence and prevent it whenever possible. It is obvious from even simple observance that all forms of life, even the tiniest bugs and parasites, strive to live. So if you value your own life, then you should respect the right of all other forms of life to live as well.

Killing is the very source of brutality and cruelty. Even killing bugs or mosquitoes with insecticides or by swatting them incites cruelty deep within our hearts. According to Buddhism, even killing insects harms the seeds of compassion within our own hearts. Considering the human being as "master of all" is not referring to our brutal strength or to our outstanding wisdom; it refers to our ability to love and to extend compassion to all forms of life. Thus there is no greater evil in Buddhism than killing something that strives to live, something that cherishes its own life just as we cherish our own.

The second training precept is refraining from taking what does not belong to you, but this does not refer solely to robbery, larceny, and petty theft. It also includes not giving. Few things could be worse than actually stealing something from someone in dire straights who works like a horse just to survive; but one thing worse is a business person who ignores labor conditions, underpays workers while living high off the hog himself, and ignores the suffering of others. And in Bodhisattvayana, the greatest non-good is not giving that which is asked of you.

Third, lay Buddhists take it upon themselves to train not only in speaking honestly but in refraining from being two-faced, from using dirty or damning language, and from unnecessary exaggeration—in other words, from any kind of verbal misconduct whatsoever. Proper and honest verbal karma is essential to developing a clear mind.

The fourth precept is to refrain from adultery. In basic Buddhism the terminology used for monks was to refrain from "sexual misconduct" of any kind, but to accommodate the laity as the Mahayana movement grew, the terminology was changed to "adultery."Adultery violates both love and trust. It is turning one's back on innate human goodness and the results can be devastating not only to social order; the perpetrator also eventually becomes his own victim. We do not have to read the daily newspapers to see what adultery can result in.

And the fifth precept is to refrain from mind-altering substances such as alcohol. Alcohol in itself is not necessarily evil and sometimes it can even be medicinal. It can help to cheer up a burdened, melancholy heart, and, in a cozy atmosphere, it can help contribute to reconciliation. The evil of alcohol is not in one drink. But one drink usually leads to another and to another, and in the process this leads to letting down one's guard, and eventually to recklessness, carelessness, vengeful acts, deadly traffic accidents, and many other misfortunes. Buddhism does not advise abstention because it wants to spoil the party. The disadvantages far outweigh the advantages of drinking, and one of the main disadvantages is that it clouds both our minds and our hearts. Just look around at the misery drinking creates today; and try to imagine the incomprehensible misery that it has created for humankind throughout history.

Opening and Closing the Window

The issue of drinking comes up even in the early sutras. The Buddha heard of a monk who had tried everything to cure an ailment but nothing worked; finally the doctor recommended limited amounts of alcohol. But the monk, having taken the Precepts in front of the Buddha, refused to violate the Precepts by taking alcohol. Upon hearing this, the Buddha went to visit the ailing monk and he spoke about alcohol.

"I have asked you all not to drink because of the damage that it can do to your body and mind. But if alcohol in some cases can be medicinal, then by all means you should take it as such in order to get well."

This is a fine demonstration of the interpretation of the Precepts. The Precepts are not windows that shut things out completely. Windows sometimes should be opened to let in fresh air. Of course, in totality, the Precepts have great meaning, but you should also develop the wisdom to know when to keep them and when not to. In Buddhism this is referred to as "the law of opening and closing," like opening and closing a window. There are no absolutes. You should develop the wisdom to decide when to open the window and when to close it.

Good and Evil in Zen

The question of "good and evil" is a highly complicated one in Buddhism, and interpretation varies according to one's level of understanding. To summarize, a basic teaching is that if you can't do good, then at least don't do evil. Another early teaching to be found is "Do good, don't do evil." Yet another interpretation is "Transcend the duality of good and evil," and another is "Avoid both good and evil."

These last two may seem contradictory, but a fundamental Buddhist teaching is that once you reach the stage of being beyond attachments and fixations, your behavior becomes one with the goodness that is beyond the duality of "good" and "bad." At that stage, you automatically assume the proper perspective on everything and move about freely, since that is the stage of liberation.

In the Platform Sutra by the Sixth Patriarch of Zen Buddhism, Master Huineng (? – 867CE), we find an interesting story concerning this teaching.

When Master Huineng was traveling south after receiving Zen transmission and the robe and bowl that went with it, he realized that a band of thugs was following him to steal these treasures from him. Among the thugs was a monk named Huiming who had been a high-ranking general in his pre-Buddhist military life. When Huiming was getting almost close enough to attack him, Master Huineng placed the robe and bowl on a boulder and yelled, "Why are you trying to take this robe and bowl from me? They are nothing but symbols."

Then he stepped back and hid behind the boulders.

When Huiming got to the robe and bowl, he tried to pick them up but they wouldn't budge. Startled into repentance, Huiming cried out, "I didn't come for the robe and bowl, I came for the Dharma!"

Huineng stepped out from behind the boulders and said, "Since you came for the Dharma, I will teach you. Now simply refrain from thinking of anything. Just keep your mind completely blank." After Huiming did this for a considerable amount of time, Huineng added, "When you are not thinking of either good or evil, do you see your original nature?"

In that instant, Huiming became enlightened.

"Don't think of good, don't think of evil" does not mean that you should pretend that you never heard of them; nor does it mean to totally disregard them. It means not to cling to the idea of them as an absolute duality. When you cling to neither good nor evil in this way, you can open the true eye of wisdom.

According to Buddhism, people are originally pure but we have been conditioned into ignorance. However, once we rid ourselves of all fixations and concepts, we can once again return to that purity and goodness, the state of total liberation.

So Buddhist practice is neither the process of gaining something nor becoming something. It is the process of emptying one's heart and regaining that original state of purity. Once we empty our hearts, we see that we already have everything. In other words, we become followers of the Way so that we can regain our original purity of heart.

"Don't think of good, don't think of evil!" *(1978)*

51. The Goddess Sisters

We're having a strong storm today. Rain is pounding onto the open porch of the hermitage and sometimes it even sounds like sand pelting on the windows. I stepped out to bring in the footwear from in front of the door and watched as the storm made a messy hairdo out of the top of the bamboo grove.

Stormy days like this on the mountain are no fun at all. I don't feel like working and my disposition starts to go down the drain. I don't feel like cooking. The birds are silent. There is only the sound of the lashing wind and rain. If the rest of my life were to be spent in days like this, I'd gladly turn in whatever time I had remaining and resign from the world.

But, then again, everything is transitory. There is nothing in the world that is constant, continuous, unchanging. If something good happens, something bad invariably follows. A cloudy or stormy day is followed by sunshine. A difficult life when young can be the price you have to pay for a happy life later. If I want to look out to the bright sunshine and open vista from the mountaintop, I have to put up with days like today. The price of the warmth of the sun is thunderstorms. The price of a beautiful rose can be a prick from one of its thorns.

On days like today, I feel like I'm on an island surrounded by a vast ocean rather than on a mountain.

Once a stranger came by and asked me why on earth I was living alone up on a mountain like this. On days like today I can understand what he meant. What fun am I getting out of life? I suppose people have to find some fun in life, but I don't really know if that's so. I just know that I'm definitely trying to live the way I want to while deriving pleasure out of little things. And I am grateful for this chance to have time with the really gentle things in life.

It could be much easier and more comfortable to go down and live in the main temple with the others. No need to worry about food or firewood. And the weather would be of no consequence. There's more to eat when you're in a group, and it's easy to get by affably. The one disadvantage of living in a group, of course, is that you can't live the way you want to. I can't feel the solitude and the lightness that I do when I live alone. The solitude, however, is not loneliness. It's more like the naked reality of existence.

Also when you're alone, you don't get caught up in the arguments that inevitably grow out of communal living. Of course, there are hardships involved in living alone, too. For example, unexpected, uninvited guests can be irksome at times. However this is part of the price I have to pay for living the way I want to, away from it all.

When I am alone I can be my genuine self, my warm self. But when you live with someone else, you can only be partially yourself.

Another reason for living alone, although it may sound paradoxical, is so that I can love everyone else. In Leo Tolstoy's most religious work, the *Brothers Karamazov*, Ivan tells his younger brother Alyosha that even if people can love someone far away, they can never love someone close by. He added that loving others required that they be out of sight and that as soon as that object of love appears, love starts to disappear.

Last summer I had a bad back problem during the rainy season. Every time I tried to get up, I felt like my back was going to snap. I had to use a cane to get into the kitchen to cook and eat, and I had a really tough time lighting fires, going to the well to fetch water, and going to the outhouse. Finally I got through it, feeling that this was part of the price I had to pay for the solitude and lightheartedness that I enjoy when living alone.

The joy of getting better always follows sickness. The body is unpredictable and unreliable, and we can't expect to be healthy all the time. Since getting sick is inevitable, think of the benefits: It affords you the opportunity to concentrate more on your health and it also provides you with a chance to get what probably is some much-needed rest.

There are two sides to every coin. If there are benefits, there are detractions; if there is good, there is also bad hiding in the shade. The problem is that it's almost human instinct to just want the good things and try to deny or avoid the unfavorable. This is both unbalanced and egocentric. Everything has a price, and there is no such thing as a free lunch.

There's an interesting parable about this in the Mahaparanirvana Sutra:

> Once there was a very beautiful woman standing in front of a man's house. He went out and asked her who she was.

> She told him that she was the Goddess of Prosperity and that, wherever she went, she bestowed wealth and riches and blessings. He invited her into his house, lit incense, sprinkled petals, and made offerings to her.
>
> Then he noticed that there was another woman standing out in front of the house. She was ugly and dressed in rags. He went out and asked her what she was doing there.
>
> She replied that she was the Goddess of Poverty and that, wherever she went, she brought bad luck and poverty with her. The man screamed at her and told her to go away. But she added, "The woman in your house is my sister and we promised each other that we would always live together. So if you drive me away, my sister will follow."
>
> The man went back in and asked the Goddess of Prosperity if that was true, and she replied that it was. She told him that if he liked her, then he would have to like her sister just as much.

The sutra goes on to tell us that the man sent them both away. Birth and death, storms and sunshine, prosperity and poverty, sunrise and sunset. You can't have one without the other. But there's a deeper meaning as well for those seeking enlightenment. Like the man in the story, free yourself of attachments to all of them. *(1982)*

52. The Winter Forest

When the winter winds begin to blow, the leaves and fruits all whirl to the ground, and the deciduous trees have nothing to show but their bare branches. At sunset, as I walk along the leaf-strewn path in the woods, I suddenly find myself reflecting on where my life is going. Then I get a bit depressed when thinking about the allotted time that has already slipped by and whether I had made the most of it.

I'm a little careful when I step on the fallen leaves. I feel that even though they are strewn all about, there is still meaning to each one's existence. It's natural law that even they have their own order and world even though we may not be able to perceive it. They exist because everything in the world is necessary to the world.

Last fall, in order to make up for my extended silence, I left the mountains and busied myself, traveling from town to town and talking to people. When I got back to the hermitage, the foliage had not only turned; much of it had already glided to the ground. For a time I had forgotten the sound of the night winds passing through the forest, but hearing them again brought the garden of my heart back to life. It was an inner journey of peace and quiet.

The mountain winds affect much more than the ears. It's as if they even blow away the dust buried deep within my bones and flowing through my veins. The sound of the mountain winds calms and clears my mind, leaving it as clean as a freshly swept yard. The winds blow away all the pollution accumulated in the cities, and bring with them the trouble-free world of an innocent heart back to me.

The wind is an invisible and evasive wanderer and, as such, it lives and moves forever. It also brings vitality to whatever it touches. I wonder what the world would be like without wind. Everything alive would probably just wither, become pallid, and choke to death.

Can we really say that something we can't see or grasp with our hands doesn't exist? Things we can see exist because there are things that we can't see, and things that we hear exist because there are things that we can't hear.

The Indian Guru Rajneesh once expressed it this way:

> A spilled drop or water makes the whole cosmos thirsty.
> Picking a flower is picking a part of the universe.
> A blossoming flower makes innumerable stars twinkle.
> It is through such interaction that everything in the
> world comes about.

Nowadays, of the many people who come up the mountain, some who sit on the porch and look down at the mountain below ask why it is so quiet here, or even worse, they say that they can't stand the quiet. They become uneasy, as if something were chasing them. Of course, these people are clever, bright people from the cities. In other words, they're urbanites who have become bound to the world of concepts. They're people who have become completely addicted to the confusion, the complexity, and the noise of urban life, people who have completely forgotten natural order and quiet. They're incapable of going somewhere and genuinely enjoying time by themselves. They can't stand on their own without expectations of something. They can't just be.

And since they can't endure the quiet of nature, they drown out the trickles of the streams and the clear, transparent songs of the birds with transistor radios. Some even bellow amid the mountains in an attempt to overcome their uneasiness. It's beyond me how such people can be considered lords of all creation. No longer even aware of who they are, modern people are becoming stranger and stranger.

In today's world, why are we so dependent on things that are visible, audible, and tangible? We've become slaves. How could we utter human words if silence didn't exist? How could there be land without the oceans? The real cannot exist without the unreal, the tangible without the intangible.

There's a line from the Diamond Sutra that explains that all phenomena, including what we see and hear and touch, are false in themselves, and that we have to be able to see both phenomena and their underlying nature at the same time if we wish to understand the real nature of the universe. In other words, we have to penetrate behind the phenomena to truly understand them.

* * * *

A number of rabbits and pheasants live around the hermitage and they are not at all surprised when they see me, perhaps because they know I won't hurt them. Sometimes after a heavy snow, I'll put out beans and other food for them, and they'll come over and eat to their hearts' content right in front of me. I become filled with a certain warmth as I watch them. Yet when people from the village down below come up, they're delighted to see peasants or rabbits wandering around the yard, mainly because they're envisioning them in a pot or on a table. Some people haven't the faintest notion of treating other forms of life as neighbors, or of teaching them to trust people. Some people can be wilder than wildlife. Fortunately, however, the innocent creatures have a strong intuitive sense.

It's early December, and at the edge of the forest stand two trees with persimmons drooping from them and they'll probably continue to droop until they fall with the first real cold spell. Pheasants and other birds have nibbled away half of them, but the rest are still in good form. People, smacking their lips, have already started asking me why I haven't picked the persimmons. I haven't told them that I know a secret: Persimmons can be eaten with the eyes as well as with the mouth.

Actually, there are two reasons why I have left the persimmons on the trees. For one thing, I really don't have much of anything else to offer the birds that come by. In addition, several times a day I derive immense joy from gazing up at the bright orange persimmons drooping below the pure blue sky of early winter.

People who have seen the color of persimmons hanging from bare branches when snow has fallen understand, even if it's just a background of snow on the mountain across the way. The combination of colors is absolutely breathtaking. One year a renowned senior monk from the big temple down the mountain used to slip and slide his way up the snowy slope just to see that entrancing color combination. It's an unmatchable sight.

If I had picked and eaten all the persimmons, how could my eyes ever have tingled with the taste of them?

In winter, the trees reveal their basic, unadorned, unpretentious nature and appearance. The forest knows that this is a kind of visual silence and it understands the meaning. It's part of the process to allow the forest, in the early spring, to bashfully stir into a new gown of green, and in the summer, to intercept the blazing rays of the sun so as to cool the earth below. Then in the fall, as their fruits ripen, the trees in the valleys seemingly point to one another's colorful gown before the leaves reluctantly fall to the ground. Then, with their heads and arms raised in the air, the trees fall into silent contemplation.

To constantly re-create oneself is to really live. The selfless Self continues to build confidence in that self. It's when such creative efforts halt that, be it a tree or a person, one beckons aging, sickness and death.

Although they appear to be just standing there mute and expressionless, trees never cease in their creative internal efforts. They turn their ears to the secret whispers of the earth and prepare for new spring growth. And then, when the time comes, they demonstrate to the world their unmitigated will to live. *(1982)*

53. Waters Flow and Flowers Blossom

During China's Tang dynasty, there was a monk, Zen Master Niaogua (Little Bird), who lived on the branches of a tree beside a magpie nest. Since he and the magpies got along so well, he came to be called Quechao, or Magpie Nest.

Since Zen monks strive to live unfettered, totally natural lives, they prefer natural settings to human settlements and cities. In warmer climates, they might live in a cave or on top of a huge boulder. Even some of the names of Zen predecessors, such as "Rock Head" and "Boulder Head," indicate the commitment to natural settings. But even setting up a place deep in the mountains results in a certain degree of attachment. To become totally free of delusions one has to become free of fetters to freedom, since all fetters, and consequently suffering, arise out of attachments.

Another reason why Zen monks prefer living with nature is that life in an artificial environment makes it easy to fall into human thought patterns that are either useless or conceptual. When you live in nature with trees or boulders or along the winding waters, your mind becomes wide-open as you gaze upon the reality of the universe.

Urbanization and industrialization demand that religions to some degree have to adapt to the changing times. However, it's good to see that the Zen monk traditions are still in fine shape despite the changing times. Between three-month meditation sessions, monks with no more than a backpack still wander aimlessly from temple to temple and from mountain to mountain like migratory birds, making progress along the Path as they go. From this perspective, it's easy to understand that Zen is dedicated to seeking truth rather than dedicated to propagation.

Hearts that have been emptied of all selfishness communicate easily. Spotless hearts make interspecific communication possible, like people and birds living together in trees. St. Francis of Assisi was a perfect example of living along nature's lines. Birds alighting on his arms and shoulders were proof of the mutual trust that spotless hearts have.

Concerning Monk Magpie Nest, one day an important government official, who was also somewhat renowned as a poet, came to ask him something.

"What is the true meaning of Buddhism?" he asked.

"Don't do evil. Do good," answered Magpie Nest.

That was hardly the answer that a prominent government official, who had taken the time to seek out the monk, had expected. He felt let down. It was a simple answer that anyone in secular society could have given him. He had hoped for a much deeper answer concerning basic Buddhist mentality. He shouted back,

"Even a three-year-old child knows that!"

The monk replied, quite seriously, "Yes, all the three-year-olds know that, but even an eighty-year-old finds it difficult to practice."

Those words really struck home with the official. He performed a full prostration to the monk and left. The lesson was easy enough: Actions have to match what you say. Merely knowing something is worthless unless you put it into practice. It's one thing to understand the principles of something, but it takes repeated efforts and training to make it part of your program.

The Buddha's teachings number more than eighty thousand but out of all those, telling a high-ranking official to rule the people virtuously rather than harassing them with injustices was the perfect answer to the question. The monk was doing something that the Buddha himself was renowned for—tailoring his teachings to the audience at hand.

The basic premise of both religions and societies in general is that actions are more important than words. Actualizing wisdom and love and virtue are essential. And in Zen Buddhism, if a person experiences ultimate truth, it is a duty to spread this truth around. That is real Dharma and real truth, and the meaning of "returning to the marketplace" in

Zen's *Ox Herding* series of paintings. Wagging the tongue without doing a thing to actualize the truth is neither Zen nor religion. If Zen stopped at enlightenment, then it would amount to nothing more than philosophy. However, Zen can become true religion because the great compassionate heart is to be found within.

Genuine Zen, rather than existing on the tongue, is demonstrated physically. It's living from moment to moment, displaying one's true nature through one's actions, living in the here and the now.

It's one thing to say that you should avoid evil and do good and another thing to actualize it. There are plenty of things in life to be grateful for, but there are plenty of traps as well. And if we aren't fully conscious all the time and if we don't know how to control our hearts, we never know when we'll fall into a trap. We have to be fully aware of where we stand all the time if we are going to avoid evil and do good.

Even in the most remote mountains where people have never been, waters flow and flowers blossom. *(1982)*

54. The Importance of Vows

Our days are filled pretty much with the same routines. We open our eyes at a certain time and we close them at a certain time, and in between we do pretty much the same things day in and day out. And we'll probably do the same things again tomorrow. I actually think that we're kind of courageous to keep living such lives with so few complaints and so little dissatisfaction.

But the same repetitive routines and habits are apt to make us indolent and incompetent. We not only get caught in a cyclic environment, we become part of it. And once we're caught in that cyclic environment, it becomes necessary for us to restructure our lives.

If we wish to live like genuine people, we have to lead innovative, creative lives. Otherwise, there's not much difference between the animal kingdom and us. But we can continue to grow through continual change. So it becomes necessary for us to live each moment and each day in the quest to become something. Life is not a goal in itself; it's the process of heading toward a goal. The journey, rather than the destination, is important. After all, aren't we all wayfarers? And since we are on the road, we have to establish a direction in which to head. Without direction we can easily become confused and lost.

Think about the past. When we had no definite direction, how much time did we waste by not being able to distinguish between what had to be done and what didn't? Didn't we just go with the flow, bending this way and that way, dependent upon others? Unable to define our own independence, how much time did we spend being pushed around by someone else or being carried away by something irrelevant? All because we hadn't set our own goal.

In Buddhist terms we would use the word "vow"instead of "goal."

Greed is necessarily personal. But Buddhist wishes and vows are altruistic, since they necessarily involve others. Of course, everyone has hopes, but if those hopes are limited to oneself or one's family, they are, to the Buddhist way of thinking, selfish. To a Buddhist, a genuine wish is one that goes beyond the personal realm to include neighbors, society, the world and even all beings throughout all the universes. For example, "May all beings be well and happy."

In Buddhism there are different kinds of wishes, hopes, and prayers. And there are vows, vows to work toward something for others. All the buddhas and bodhisattvas have established great vows for the benefit of all beings. Amitabha, the Buddha of Infinite Light, has forty eight vows, the Healing Buddha twelve, and the Bodhisattva of Universal Practice, Samantabadhra, ten. Such great vows can be found throughout Buddhism. Ksitigarbha is the Bodhisattva of Rescue who vows not to become enlightened himself until all beings are rescued from hellish torments. This typifies the bodhisattva ideal.

The buddhas and bodhisattvas were all born through the power of great vows, while sentient beings like us are born out of the power of karma from past deeds. These principles do not apply just to birth, however. Indeed, the buddhas and bodhisattvas continue through the power of their vows just as we sentient beings continue through the power of our karma. The difference is that the buddhas and bodhisattvas have independent lives, while our lives are both dependent and interdependent.

A Buddhist is someone who follows the teachings of the Buddha. So we should ask ourselves to what extent we are living independent lives. We should think about what wishes and vows we have made, and how we are trying to realize them.

A Buddhist monk isn't someone who just shaves his head and lives in a temple; nor is a lay Buddhist just someone who makes offerings and prays at a temple. Those are all formalities. It is the way that you live that determines whether you are a true practicing Buddhist or not. Someone who merely goes through the formalities cannot be considered a Buddhist.

A true Buddhist makes vows. Of the forty-eight Bodhisattva precepts, the thirty-fifth and thirty-sixth emphasize the importance of establishing vows and working toward them with great courage and determination. Vows are useless if one merely establishes them and does not strive towards their fulfillment, and the same goes for actions without a vow. Vows and actions go together like the wheels of a cart.

All Mahayana Buddhists have four vows in common, The Four Great Vows. We recite them at the end of every ceremony or gathering, but how often do we recite them out of rote, without really thinking about their true meaning? These Four Great Vows typify Mahayana altruism and concern for all forms of life.

The First Great Vow: "I vow to rescue all beings"

The First Great Vow is to rescue all beings from suffering and troubles. When you think about it, this is an incredible vow to make. We can't even rescue ourselves from suffering and troubles, so how can we vow to rescue an infinite number of sentient beings?

But in a sense we can be reborn just by making this vow, by making a commitment to all forms of life. Perhaps we have recited it an infinite number of times already, but have we really thought about it and really lived up to the vow? I, too, am embarrassed by my failure to live up to it by just paying lip service. In our daily lives it's easy for us to frequently get upset over trivialities and to argue. But by remaining conscious of this First Great Vow, we can make all sorts of improvements in our daily lives, beginning with preventing others from suffering by refraining from engaging in harmful behavior. Then gradually we can work into a more active role in eliminating the suffering of others.

Some people do in fact ask how they could possibly be capable of saving others when they haven't even rescued themselves from suffering and misery. This reflects a misunderstanding of Mahayana. Rather than working from the subjective, the Mahayana approach is the altruistic attitude of being concerned with others, rather than the self, first.

Zen Formality, a basic handbook in the theories of Zen, emphasizes the necessity of an aspiring practitioner to radiate bodhicitta, or "the mind seeking enlightenment for all." Written by the Chinese Ch'an Master Tsungtse, the book has been extensively used for ages as a primer, and begins with, "A practitioner studying wisdom must first arouse within himself great compassion and then establish a vow. One must vow, while continuing with highly intensive meditation, to lead sentient beings. One must not be committed to liberating only oneself."

Rather than trying to become liberated first and then rescuing others, the Mahayana Bodhisattva ideal is to rescue oneself by rescuing others, to liberate oneself by liberating others. Developing such a will towards enlightenment for all is essential to being a Buddhist. This vow alone can immensely enrich your monotonous daily routines.

The Second Great Vow: "I Vow To End All Suffering."

We covet and desire things beyond our reach, frequently get angry, and at times are so blind as to be unable to see even an inch in front of us. These are Buddhism's Three Poisons: avarice, anger, and foolish thinking. It's easy enough to say that we can overcome these but certainly not that easy to do. Think about how difficult it is for us to break even one bad habit.

Mental suffering in itself is neither good nor bad; how we approach the suffering determines the influence it will have upon us. Consequently, rather than trying to sever the anguish, we have to try to convert it into enlightenment, to turn the arrows into flowers. We have to learn how to convert the energy of anguish into the energy of enlightenment. We can convert the energy of greed and avarice into the energy of sharing and generosity; we can convert the energy of anger into the energy of patience and understanding; and we can convert the energy of foolishness into the energy of wisdom.

Trying to overcome anguish provides us with the opportunity to sprout the seeds of enlightenment. Thus, by taking a leap of logic, we can say that anguish in a sense is enlightenment since it can lead us there. We should be grateful for anguish.

The Third Great Vow: "I Vow To Learn All Dharma Teachings."

There are no limits to the teachings of the holy ones, since Dharma teachings are not limited to Dharma talks and the sutras. If you look carefully, you'll understand that the sound of the wind, the sound of the waters, the blossoming flowers and the singing birds—virtually everything—are all Dharma teachings. Unfortunately, many Buddhists misunderstand this point and believe that Zen, chanting, and praying are the only real Dharma teachings, while everything else is heretical. If the Buddha had thought that there was only one method to achieve enlightenment, then why did he bother delivering eighty-four thousand Dharma teachings? The Buddha taught a variety of methods to match the needs and capabilities of all people so that they could choose and concentrate on the appropriate method, come to realize their own buddha nature, and behave like awakened ones.

Followers have to study and practice until they die. By constantly listening, thinking, and behaving properly, we can deepen our daily routines and sublimate them into something useful. When people pour their total efforts into studying and practicing, they neither age, nor get sick, nor die suddenly. Aging, sickness, and sudden death come to knock on the doors of those who do not make determined, creative efforts to learn and to practice.

The Fourth Great Vow: "I Vow To Attain Enlightenment."

No matter how lofty your ideals, you can always attain them so long as you do not give up along the way. There's a saying that steadfast progress without regression is in itself realizing Buddhahood. You must become the Buddhist Way itself, and when you do, you will be able to achieve Buddhism's loftiest goals. It all depends on the strength of your vow and commitment.

There is really nothing special about existence as is. But even the most insignificant person, having established a goal and made a vow, can make incalculable progress and achieve wonders.

A person without a vow does not have the credentials to be a Buddhist, because a Buddhist without a vow cannot sprout the seed of self-awakening. By making a vow one can turn an uncertain, wilting life into one that is clear and filled with energy, and in the process reap the rewards of that life. A life without a vow is as hollow and empty as a shell.

If we are to going to continue to be reborn in a repetitious daily life, we have to establish a pure, great vow that matches our situation and our capabilities. Until now we have just gone along with everyone and everything else, only to become injured one way or another. And that is because we have not had a barometer for our lives. If we really strive to live each moment with a vow that will contribute to both personal and social benefit, then we will be able to blossom as fragrantly as the flowers. *(1983)*

55. Full Emptiness

It's winter. And it's raining. It's the season for snow, but it's raining. After nothing but the sound of sad, dry winds for weeks, the whispers of gently falling rains moisten my heart.

In the mountains, this is a perfect day to meditate. All I have to do is sit here silently and listen. No need for a koan or anything else—just an empty heart and open ears. When I turn my ears to the sounds of nature, I can take aim at washing away, particle by particle, the dust in my heart. On a day like today, if I sit quietly without being disturbed at all, I can discover the true joy of existence.

Even the most marvelous music in the world cannot match the sounds of nature, because music is the product of imperfect people, people who are naturally subject to ups and downs, contradictions, and conflicts. Consequently, artificial music, as marvelous as it can be, cannot give us the same peace of mind that the sounds of nature can. The sounds of nature are filled with life itself. They're uncontrived. They're completely harmonious.

Nature doesn't ask anything of people. Nor does it demand anything. On the other hand, people ask too much of nature, they take from it, and they ruin it. Yet nature gives whatever is asked of it. The earth is humanity's mother, and like a child snuggled in its mother's embrace, we feel secure and satisfied whenever we lean on nature. So why do we abuse it?

The detoxifier for civilization cannot be found in developing more civilization. It has to be found in what we began with in the first place, with nature. There is not a religion in the world that can provide such an eternal refuge for everyone like nature can.

Over a lifetime, we experience innumerable changes of the seasons—spring, summer, fall, and winter—over and over again. But how many times have we ever considered the benevolent meaning of each season? And not only the seasons. How many times have we really been aware of the meaning of each day, or for that matter, of each moment?

There is no guarantee that we will see the coming spring or summer, or fall or winter; we live without knowing what is going to happen tomorrow. So we should be grateful for each moment that we live, right now, right here. There is no sense in worrying about tomorrow if our lives are blossoming and bearing fruit today. Worrying about tomorrow is proof that we are not living today to the fullest. If we are making the most of today, there is no reason to fret about tomorrow.

It's winter and it's raining. It's supposed to be one of the coldest times of the year, yet there is a spring-like drizzle falling. And the forest is shrouded in fog. The winter birds are chattering in the black persimmon tree. I am nearly overcome with a sense of gratitude to everything for this tranquility and peacefulness.

I recently received a letter from someone who wrote that her son, upon hearing a tape recording of the Diamond Sutra, said, "When I listen to this tape, my heart empties. But it's not emptiness with nothing there. It's an emptiness that is filled with something, kind of like the desert: The desert looks completely empty but it's filled with an incomprehensible number of grains of sand."

That was an incredible insight. The mother said that it lit up the kitchen where they stood. Sounds that come from a pure and lucid heart make the hearts of its listeners just as pure and lucid. Since that heart is empty, it echoes, it resonates. It's like an empty earthen jar that probably feels greater satisfaction being empty than full.

There's a mysterious essence to a vacuum. Something that is completely empty is completely filled with potential. When our hearts are free of attachments and troubles, they become rich. And a rich heart clarifies our perceptions. Such a heart leads us into the world of creativity.

But how often in our daily lives do we suffer from being tied up with trivia, things, and people? Fixations bind us and interfere with our ability to fully express ourselves. We are familiar enough with that lighthearted feeling that results from breaking away from such fixations, both large and small. But even so, sometimes it doesn't work because we don't know how to use our hearts properly. If we wish to learn how, first it is imperative that we practice emptying our hearts by releasing them from the swamp of conditioned ideas.

To empty our hearts we have to be able to listen to something; and in order to do that, we have to eliminate the static of unnecessary chatter. Then, when we are alone, we have to take a good hard look at the realities of our own world.

The sounds of civilization that attract us actually distract us and disturb us, probably because they lack the essence of life. But the sounds of nature themselves are the complete harmonization of life. As such they purify and pacify the heart.

Yet the sounds of life are definitely not to be found only outside the self, such as in the sound of the wind or the sound of the water. The true basic sounds of nature are to be found welling up from within rather than from without.

Turning the ears to the sound from within is called "observation." And when you progress in observing the heart throughout your daily activities, you'll have complete self-control no matter how unruly and troublesome the outside world may become.

We have too many things now. We are too dependent on the tools and conveniences of civilization. We are wearing layer upon layer of false clothing. We eat anything and everything, and not just food. We indiscriminately devour knowledge and information and recreation and hobbies. Yet at the same time we have too many prejudices, too many reasons for everything, and too many complicated, unruly thoughts. All of this deprives us of the robustness of basic human health. And we have no one to blame for all of this but ourselves.

Rather than being found in an expensive prescription at the drugstore, true health is to be found by opening our eyes to our original condition. We have to become naked again by peeling off the layers of false clothing with which we have adorned ourselves. And to restore our basic health, we have to peel off the inner layers covering our heart as well. That is the best way to avoid that rashness and greed of trying to become something that we are not. By returning to this fundamental inner simplicity, we can see the truth of our lives and thus overcome our own contradictions and conflicts.

Listening closely to the sound of the winter rain makes me want to become even simpler. I want to become free of everything that I own. And I want to lay bare completely my true, original self. *(1983)*

56. Buddhist Rituals

A Buddhist purification ritual is a form of repentance for misdeeds. In addition, in this process of cleansing, the ritual provides the participants with the impetus to improve their tri-karma of thought, word, and action, and to work toward fulfillment of their hopes. This is also an occasion to gather all the monks at the temple together for a meal offering. It has been a very important part of Buddhism ever since the time of the Buddha. Among other things, it reflects the symbiotic relationship between the monks and the lay community.

Not so very long ago, someone came to an elderly monk at a temple, asked him to prepare such a purification ritual, and gave him a large sum of money in advance. The day before the scheduled ritual, the monk and an assistant went down to the market to buy the necessary food and supplies. When they got to the village below the temple, they came across a woman sitting on the ground with her legs stretched out and wailing away. The monk asked her what was wrong. The woman told him that she was being evicted from her home because of all of the debts she had incurred while caring for her chronically ill husband. The monk, filled with compassion for the woman, reached into his knapsack, took out all the money for the ritual and gave her all of it. He then turned around and went back to the temple.

The housekeeper at the temple had a fit since there was nothing for the ritual. The monk didn't say another word.

The people arrived the next day for the ritual and went in to greet the monk. He welcomed them warmly and then told them that he had held the ritual the day before. Understandably, the people became flustered. The monk then explained what had happened. The leader of the group, evidently a bighearted person, not only thanked the monk profusely but also gave him another sum of money as an offering, and then they all went on their way.

Many lay and even monastic Buddhists may find it hard to understand why the monk gave the ritual money to the distraught woman on the street. This incident forces us to think about the genuine meaning of how to conduct a true Buddhist ritual.

*****

Most people, when they hear the term Buddhist ritual, think of a Forty-ninth Day Reincarnation Ceremony or a 100th Day Spirit Guiding Ceremony for the deceased. The altars are filled with food offerings and the monks conduct long drawn-out sessions with percussion instruments and bells accompanied by prayers, incantations, and unfamiliar chants adapted from Sanskrit. If a temple holds a large-scale ritual, there's always great commotion, the rituals drag on, and the meal offerings are invariably late. Such events cannot be called "true Dharma rituals."

There also seems to be growing confusion among Buddhists between memorial services and Buddhist rituals. Memorial services are a type of Confucian etiquette of offering food to the spirits of ancestors. But Buddhist rituals, as mentioned, are events that cleanse one's karma and also gather the monks together for a meal offering.

In Buddhist spirit-guiding services for the deceased, the necessity of proper rituals is all the more important. And the services should be conducted in language that the laity can understand.

Before the Buddha passed into nirvana, his faithful disciple Ananda asked him what they should do with his remains. He admonished his disciples to have nothing to do with a funeral and to continue to dedicate themselves totally to their own salvation. He said that truly dedicated lay followers should handle any and all funeral arrangements. *(1983)*

57. A Letter to the Female Monks at Unmunsa Temple

Whenever I think of Unmunsa, the first thing that comes to mind is the unforgettable site from my last visit: one hundred thirty pairs of white slippers that were all lined up on the stone steps outside the Dharma Hall.

In the old days each temple had a calligraphy wood carving hanging on the front of the Dharma Hall: "Look right beneath your feet."The literal meaning was to be sure that you had taken off your footwear in the proper place. However, the deeper Zen saying, "Look right beneath your feet,"means that practitioners should repeatedly reflect upon their present reality, from moment to moment, in forming their character. If we don't remain aware, then we can easily becoming a creature of habit and routine, and our role as a monk becomes no more than just a job.

A monk training center such as Unmunsa Temple provides basic education for new practitioners of course, but you should not think that this education is limited to The Three Baskets of Buddhism—Discourses, Discipline, and Abhidharma, or "Buddhist psychology." Of course, a practitioner has to become well versed in the scriptures, but behavior is just as important. You don't have to be in a temple if your objective is just to study the scriptures. From one point of view, it is actually possible to study more logically and systematically outside the temple.

Monks cannot study properly if they don't train behaviorally as well, and that is precisely what temple training is for. The Buddha taught both The Three Baskets and methods of practice. Some may mistake a Buddhist educational site such as Unmunsa Temple as a place just for learning; however, the basic nature of religious life is not to be found merely in scriptures and theory but also in the purity of practice. Today's world, where behavior is becoming more and more unruly, demands that the Sangha's practice becomes all the more precious and pure.

A monk can form a sound character only when understanding and practice become one. Understanding without practice can easily become useless and practice that doesn't correspond to understanding can lead to blind behavior. A practitioner must have great faith in order for understanding and practice to become one. So today I would like to recommend five measures that hopefully will aid your study and practice as scholar-monks at Unmunsa Temple.

First, make your studies worthwhile. You should become familiar with a broad variety of things that will be of help to you throughout your life. Your education here is not limited to the courses you take; in fact, you have to study even harder on your own.

In addition, you have to incorporate what you learn into your daily behavior and have it become part of your character. You have to be able to show others what you have learned. It would be senseless for you to go through the motions here for five or six years and have nothing to show for it. On the basis of what you learn, you should be able to deliver Dharma talks and on occasion write. And you have to become creative with what you have studied. So please find a way to apply your education after you have finished.

Second, become a unique practitioner. We all have our own distinct capabilities and qualities as a result of karma accumulated over numerous previous existences. Rather than letting those talents go to waste, please make the most of them. If you put all your talents and qualities together, you can achieve a healthy cosmic harmony. Don't try to become like everyone else, like one in a row of products coming off an assembly line. The more you practice, the more you should be able to exhibit your own capabilities. Take a look at the flowers. Different flowers have different names for a reason: They all blossom in different ways.

Third, since you have now become a monastic, you have to rid yourself of worldly feminine ways. You have to build the karma of a mature monastic. Look at the clothes you are wearing now. They are not women's clothes; they are the clothes of a mature monastic. Each moment is said to be an expression of the life of that person, but on the other hand, that same moment is part of the process of forming your character. The character you are forming is not that of a woman in a skirt; it should be of a mother to the Earth itself, a Buddha Mother to all.

Fourth, while living among many, become patient and prudent. In the search for your Self, you need some time to yourself. As a practitioner you have to come to know the true meaning of solitude. If you don't come to know this, then it is easy for you to become tarnished. In this process you have to minimize talk. Is it possible to verbally express every thought that you have? Too much talk not only makes people scatterbrained, it also drains them.

And, finally, blossom anew every day. And don't become trapped by anything. A practitioner, like the water, should continue to flow endlessly toward the great sea. Today's flower is not the same as the one that blossomed yesterday. And a practitioner, like a flower, should blossom anew every day.

Scholar-monks are eternal seekers of the truth. Seeking truth has to become second nature to you. If you don't continue to strive to seek and if searching doesn't become second nature to you, you can fall victim to the trends of the times. Remember that every single day of your life forms your character. Stay awake and stay aware all the time. A true practitioner has to remain awake even while the rest of the world sleeps. *(1983)*

58. The Sound of Water, The Sound of Wind

While living at the hermitage up on the mountain, I used to listen to the sound of the wind. But now that I'm living down in the valley, I listen instead to the sound of water, to the stream.

The sounds of the water and the wind are both natural but each evokes different reactions. Sometimes when I listen to the sound of the wind that comes from the forest, I can feel rather hollow inside and I get the urge to just get up and go somewhere. And on days when a storm rages, I become a virtual field of troubles and loneliness.

My new quarters, however, are right beside a stream. At first, I didn't really like the constant sound of the water flowing by day and night but there was no way to avoid it. The first couple of days here were rainy, so I couldn't help but notice the increasing loudness. Now that I've gotten used to it, it doesn't bother me very much. On the contrary, since I now regard it as the sound of time and life flowing by, it has given me a new concept of time.

The water sounds quite different from the searing, dry, empty winds of winter. There's something moist and rich about it. And it sounds like it is endlessly washing something away, although I'm not quite sure what.

Now that I've come down from the mountain to the valley, I want to live a hidden life. Having lived pretty much the way I wanted all alone up there in the hermitage, I find myself wanting to lose myself in communal life again. Since I can't change the world all by myself, I want to at least be able to rearrange my own lifestyle. I want to wake up to my latent self through new changes. That's because I think that life, rather than being an end in itself, is an endless experiment, an adventure.

I had lived in the hermitage for seven and a half years. When it came time to leave, most of all I felt sorry and sad for the Buddha there. I had enshrined him for more than ten years, since my early days at an urban temple. I had brought the Buddha from a temple that had closed, but the Buddha image was still there at the abandoned temple, enshrined on a large table. The first time I saw that Buddha, I was thrilled like never before. That Buddha totally captivated me. That was a genuine meeting. I made up my mind then and there to enshrine that Buddha for my own practice. I continued to have a special fondness for that Buddha. He was not all that old but there was something elegant about the image.

When I had moved from the urban temple to the hermitage, I put all my bags in the trunk of a car, but I put the Buddha on the seat beside me. If you're going to live alone, it's easy to fall into the trap of laziness, but by enshrining the Buddha, I would be sure to be busy all day—just his presence would urge me on to make greater progress on the Way.

Having moved into the hermitage, the Buddha provided more than just motivation. He also listened to my hopes and prayers, and he put up with my tantrums and habits. Sometimes when I went down the mountain to the main temple and it got late, the other monks would badger me to stay overnight, but I always fought my way out because I felt bad about leaving the Buddha in the hermitage alone. How could I not?

Another thing that bothered me about leaving the hermitage was leaving the trees that I had planted and raised. The day I left, it seemed as if the silver magnolia, the juniper, and the ginkgo were all staring at me, disappointed, and wondering why I was leaving them.

For years we had shared the bright sunshine together and looked at the stars together. We also took in the blizzards and wild rainstorms together. In gratitude for my trimming them and fertilizing them with compost, they used to cool me off in the summer with their fresh leaves and generous shade. Living in the same compound together, we really developed affection for one another.

It's easy to feel this way when you pack your knapsack to hit the road again as a wanderer, but this time, as I packed my things one by one, I suddenly felt a hunger, a hollowness that is at the base of our existence. I wonder if—when it comes time for each one of us, alone, to leave this planet—we won't feel this same kind of emptiness when we reflect on the life that we had led.

Having moved into the valley, I spent several days busily getting my new place in order to my liking. There were the electric repairs and wallpapering to do. I also had to put in new piping and place large stones at the well for doing the laundry. I replaced the fuel hole for cooking and heating water but it didn't work well when I tried to light a fire. I took it apart and redid it, and finally the fire burned fitfully. I heightened the chimney, which in the temple we refer to as the "wood smoke pagoda" since we burn wood for fuel. Then I cut a few bamboos from the bamboo grove to make poles for clotheslines. And I replaced and heightened the slats for squatting in the outhouse.

Inside, I hammered two large bamboo nails into the wall to hang my robes, and by putting a fresh camellia branch into a white vase, I transformed the room into a spring setting. I also hung a calligraphy scroll on the wall with a saying by the Chinese Ch'an Master Linchi—"There is only now." The place suddenly felt like home.

"There is only now." Once something is past, it's past, and there's no sense in fretting about the future. Every time I look at these words, I become freshly inspired to live each moment to the utmost. We live in the now. And if you can live to the fullest in each successive now, you can live a life of no regrets.

It's getting late. It has already been some time since they sounded the large bell. I'm again listening to the sound of water in the night.

It almost sounds like falling rain. It doesn't rest for a second. It just continues to flow and flow on its way to becoming one with the distant ocean. Our lives, too, are flowing inexorably toward becoming one with the ocean. *(1983)*

59. Under the Stars

At the hermitage, I used to spend summer evenings out in the yard in front. It was stuffy inside and if I turned on a light, an influx of insects would have a fine time dancing around it and mistaking me for a buffet. So I rolled out a mat in the yard and spent my evenings there. From there I could greet the moon rising majestically over the faint ridge across the way: I used to welcome this silent blessing of the Moonlight Bodhisattva with palms together and bowing in humble greeting.

It's difficult to go to sleep on a bright moonlit night, probably because of our subtle sensitivities, which can be as delicate as the moonlight itself.

It's much more dazzling to watch the stars when you're comfortably stretched out than it is if you're sitting. On a perfectly clear night, as you stare at the infinite number of stars across the sky, you can't help but be awestruck by the mystical, boundless universe.

As I stared at the sky studded with these endless jewels, I returned to my childhood. It's fun to search out the constellations that I had learned early on and to pick out such valuable gifts to the early navigators as the Big Dipper and the North Star. One of the easiest planets to spot in the summer sky is Mars. Photos sent back by Viking 1 in 1976 revealed not much more than stretches of rock, but on a summer night from Earth, Mars can be the brightest star in the sky. As we pass the seventh day of the seventh lunar month every year, Altair and Vega, the two love stars, are gradually separating. Vega is still bright but Altair is starting to fade as the Eagle stands guard behind him.

If you know how to spot a number of stars and constellations, the night sky seems much friendlier. It's like moving to a new town—it's much easier to come to like a place if you already have a friend there.

There's something fresh and light about using the name of a flower or a star or a tree because they can invoke a garden or a forest or a constellation in our hearts.

A famous Korean poet, Kim Chunsu, expressed this in his poem "Flowers":

> Before I called its name,
> It was little more than just something there.
> But once I called its name,
> It came to me as a flower.

The poem reflects rapport between the poet and the flower. Every day we come into contact with innumerable things, but since we don't even know their names we often don't know how to appreciate them. So we just pass them off as nothing more than "just something there." They become no more than strangers to us. Today, even all the stars of stage and screen and sports—regardless of their given natural names—avoid using names of flowers or trees or stars as they did before. This, too, reflects how we continue to distance ourselves from nature.

If we wish to establish a rapport with the worlds of flowers or stars, then we have to come to know the meaning of silence. And that necessitates remaining silent. One of the tragedies of contemporary people is that they have lost the art of complete silence. We always have to make a fuss about something and can't seem to ever keep our mouths still. Flowers and stars are, in themselves, the worlds of silence. So, if you don't understand the meaning of silence, you can't see their essence.

Religious beliefs also mature in silence. The holy ones, in both the East and the West, have always grown through silence. But nowadays it seems that religious people, both ordained and lay, have much too much to say.

It takes patience to come to know silence. In order to limit the flow of words to those with meaning, you have to learn to swallow rather than spew out meaningless talk. Words that help neither the speaker nor the listener are no more than a form of noise pollution. A sound can echo only where there is silence, only where it can echo. When people are really communicating, there has to be silence as well as talk. That silence leads to a genuine heart.

People who truly love each other don't really need words. Silence, rather than noisy talk, indicates a deep love. In contrast to the Western custom of frequently saying, "I love you," we traditionally consider it a much deeper devotion to express love silently, with a soft touch, with a pat, or just by abiding quietly at a slight distance.

Once the dog days of summer are over and the first vibrations of autumnal energy begin to seep in, the crickets and other night bugs take up their choruses at full throttle. Listening to them, I suddenly realize that they're not much different from us in their noise.

When you look out to the vast and boundless universe of stars, you take on a new perspective, one of realizing that in this vast, endless universe, a single person is no more than a speck of dust and that much of our own noise is so unnecessary.

The art of silence fills the garden of your heart with silence. *(1984)*

60. Compassion as Tathagata

Tathagata means "one thus come from the world of truth." When we awaken to compassion, we are living the truth and are taking a step toward becoming a Tathagata. The following is a quote from the Mahaparinirvana Sutra:

> A bodhisattva gives selflessly without thought of fame or profit, or deceiving others. One must neither be proud of giving nor expect something in return. When offering, we must have no thoughts of the giver or receiver. In genuine giving, we never consider the recipient or what happens after the act. Since this type of offering is the first of the Six Perfections, we must practice it in order to become enlightened.
>
> In offering something, a bodhisattva considers all beings with equal compassion and thinks of all as one's own children. A bodhisattva cares for the sick in the same way that a parent cares for a sick child. When seeing others filled with happiness,

> a bodhisattva is as happy as a parent seeing a child recover from an illness. And after offering something, a bodhisattva is as relieved as parents letting a full-grown children go out on their own.

Most people think of generosity as giving, but a more appropriate term would be "sharing."Giving implies that you have something of your own. But nothing is ours. Everything is a temporary gift from the universe. So rather than giving, we share what the universe has lent us.

Charity is usually vertical but sharing is horizontal. And it is through sharing that we can bond with other people. That is why the First Perfection *(Paramita)* is selfless giving, offering, sharing. Paramita means "to reach the other shore,"or nirvana. Through selflessness we can perfect sharing and by perfecting all Six Paramita we can reach the other shore.

*****

Outside factors and environment may provide some limits to our freedom, but from the Buddhist perspective, the causes of our limitations are ones that we have created ourselves through the Three Poisons of avarice, anger, and delusion. The problem becomes one of how to eliminate these poisons.

Selfless sharing is the way to overcome greed, desire, and coveting. The psychology is that greed and coveting melt away when you become concerned only with sharing.

Some ask how you can selflessly share when you don't have anything. Others wonder whether or not they'll wind up as beggars by sharing what they have, and perhaps it seems that way superficially. But we have a lot more to share than you may first think we do. We have a well that never goes dry, no matter how much we siphon out of it. And the deeper you go the clearer and more beautiful this bottomless well gets.

Take a look around you and see if your corners are filled with things that you really don't need. Think of the time you spend engrossed in putting this here and that there. Then think of what you could have done with those things and that time.

But materials aren't the only things we have. Our hearts are inexhaustible storehouses. The only problem is that we keep them locked up. By sharing things in our heart one by one, we get to unlock and open the door to the heart bit by bit. And it is by fully opening up the heart that we become truly human and fully free.

When you share, don't think of yourself or of the receiver. If you think of yourself, you can't open your heart fully. If you worry ahead of time that whatever it is you are sharing should really go to your family, then you wind up closing the door to your heart again.

In general, people like to share with those they are fond of but not with those they dislike. This is precisely what we have to overcome. Delusion is the source of such discrimination.

Our original heart is wide-open, but the delusions and discriminations of the mind and their resulting conflicts close the door to this heart and prevent us from being free and at peace. Sharing helps us to build confidence. If there were no one to share with, then there would be no way for us to open up our hearts.

The sutras all state that genuine giving, or sharing, is done without thought of three things: the giver, the receiver, and the gift itself. In addition, we should not think of what the receiver does with what we gave—our karma ends with the act of sharing. Sharing should be your only concern, so do not wonder whether the receiver is grateful. Wanting recognition or gratitude ruins the act. It's like inviting your opening heart to close up again.

We are all wayfarers who come into this world empty-handed and leave empty-handed. We can't take a single thing with us. Kahlil Gibran, in *The Prophet*, said, "All that you have someday shall be given. Therefore give now, that the season of giving may be yours and not your inheritor's."

A fear of need ahead of time indicates a heart that is needy. You should realize that by sharing you are gaining more in the sense that you are bonding with others.

The Mahaparinirvana Sutra continues:

> Compassion is the basis for all buddhas and bodhisattvas. A bodhisattva can perform unlimited kindness once compassion arises in the heart. Should people ask you the basis for kindness,

> just tell them it's compassion. Kindness rises out of sincerity, and sincere compassion is never futile. Sincerity of thought is compassion, and compassion is the Tathagata.

Again, Tathagata means "one thus come from the world of truth." When we awaken to compassion, we are living the truth and are taking a step towards becoming a Tathagata. *(1984)*

61. Practicing the Precepts

A few days ago, there was a newspaper article about a taxi driver who returned a large sum of money to its owner who had left it in his cab. The driver had spent the night before wondering which would get the best of him, temptation or conscience, and his conscience won out. Of course, it is the duty of a driver to return something that was left in his vehicle, but still everyone found it quite moving that he had.

It's easy to talk about it, but who wouldn't have had a conflict between keeping and returning such a sum of money? Finally, the driver empathized with the owner's predicament so he reported the loss to the proper authorities, who in turn located the owner.

Robbery is not limited to taking something from someone else's home. Many of the sutras mention the fact that not giving what is asked is just as much a form of thievery as is stealing. There's no such thing as a free lunch in this world, and you reap what you sow. If you don't plant, you'll have nothing to reap. In addition, a sudden windfall will often be followed, sooner or later, by a sudden fallout. These are the principles of the universe and the laws of cause-and-effect.

In our daily lives we are tempted by many things in many ways, even if it's not a large sum of cash like the taxi driver found. And temptation becomes greater if no one is looking. I'm embarrassed to say that once in my life I once removed unmarked postage stamps from one envelope to reuse on another. Of course, it was a time when we were really hurting for everything, including the price of a stamp or two.

But each of us has to have a set of standards and discipline if we want order in our lives. If we don't have standards and discipline, we can easily fall victim to the endless temptations that confront us.

A poor person who has his own standards retains human dignity and poise. On the other hand, someone well-off who has no standards or principles will never be able to reap the benefits of human morality.

Just as each house has its own motto, its own principles, and its own traditions, each religion has its own codes of behavior. And that's what commandments and precepts are all about.

The basic Buddhist training precepts are the Five Lay Precepts, namely, to refrain from taking life in any form, from taking what doesn't belong to one, from lying, from adultery, and from drunkenness. So a Buddhist is one who has taken refuge in the Three Jewels of the Buddha, the Dharma, and the Sangha, and who takes and tries to keep the basic precepts. Once one has formally taken the precepts, he or she should always try to abide by them.

One of the things that distinguishes people from animals is the ability to make and keep vows and promises. And it's such standards of behavior that help to improve the quality of our lives. Vows and promises help to keep our potentially fickle minds from wavering, and once we have stability in this sense, we can begin to see more clearly.

Nowadays people compare the precepts to a dish, meditation to water, and wisdom to the moon. A broken dish cannot hold water. A dish has to be complete to hold water, and the water has to be clear for the moon to shine in it.

These three things are called the "Three Baskets"of Buddhism—discipline, meditation, and wisdom. Different Buddhist sects may have different practices, but all come from the same basic framework of the Three Baskets. And even though each of the three baskets is separate, there is a deep, intrinsic relationship among all of them. If one doesn't practice the purity of the precepts, then one can't achieve proper concentration and meditation, and without proper meditation, one cannot achieve proper wisdom.

Some may ask what difference it makes if a person gets drunk and makes merry once in awhile, but that is nothing more than a cop-out. Proper awakening is impossible if one's practice is imperfect. Once people realize this, they will modify their behavior.

We all have to be aware that realizing religious truth isn't born out of lip service; it's something that has to be realized by constantly purifying our tri-karma of thought, word, and behavior. The problems that face Buddhism today are the result of the fact that people, both lay and monastic, only pay lip service to the Three Baskets and fail to practice as they should.

One needs healthy standards to lead a healthy life. And actualizing the precepts is more important than just taking them in a ceremony. Rather than running from temple to temple every year to take the Bodhisattva Precepts over and over to make merit or whatever, it's time for us to really think about how we are conducting our daily lives. *(1984)*

62. "Empty Heart Stream"

Did you ever notice that flowers bloom when it's time to bloom and wither when it's time to wither? And they do it all without a second thought. They simply display what they are—their colors, their fragrances, their shapes. Unlike people, they don't envy one another; they don't speak ill of one another; and they don't flaunt themselves. They just do what they are, effortlessly, silently. And by doing so, they brighten everything around them.

But as people, we don't have a day of peace. We are so overwhelmed by so many things that we don't even have the freedom to choose anymore. Yet we continue to look at and listen to things we don't need to, cluttering our minds and hearts. We also buy things that we hardly need, indicating that we are losing control over our own hearts.

It has been quite some time since we've forgotten how to look at the flowers, to listen to the sounds, and to watch the waters flow. Instead, we keep trying to make our lives busier and busier. We've reached the state where we are more familiar with the sound of machines than we are with the sounds of nature—the sound of water and the sound of wind. As if the noises that exhaust and annoy us everyday weren't enough, we now add to them with the loud, dizzying noises of electronic games. We are the children of the culture of machines.

We need empty hearts, hearts that are free of the greed of the world. Our original heart is the empty heart. This original heart doesn't try to fill itself up; it simply resonates as it should. A heart that cannot resonate causes us to flop, to become impotent, to wither.

Recently I went to a city that has a large stream running through it. Actually it's more like a river but it is called "No Heart Stream," that is, the "empty heart stream." It flows without thinking; it flows like an empty heart. What a fantastic name for a river. If the stream flowed like a person, with all kinds of biases, discriminations, and preconceptions, it would get caught along the way and would not be able to flow to the sea. It would stop flowing and the water would stagnate. But because a river just flows, it passes mountains and valleys, and fields and paddies, and then it finally reaches the ocean. It has to enter that ocean of life in order to move like the waves and to live eternally.

The shadow of the bamboo grove in the moonlight
Moves like a sweeping broom,
Yet not a spot of dust is swept away.
The moon reflects deep into the pond,
Yet there's not even a trace of it
On top of the water.

(1984)

63. The Mentality of Meditation

The ninth century Chinese Ch'an Master Linchi (?-866CE) studied under a very strict master, Huangp'o Siyin (?-850CE), near Mt. Huangp'o, and became enlightened. Sometime thereafter, Master Linchi decided to return to a place near his hometown. So Master Huangp'o decided to present him with certificates of ordination and transmission, which were the only two material things of importance in Zen. Master Linchi took them, and then yelled to an assistant to bring a torch so that he could burn them.

This was cutting to the heart of Zen with a sudden and dramatic rejection of worldly convention. The meaning, of course, was that it's the actual opening of the eye that is important, not physical proof. This demonstrated Master Linchi's total rejection of any kind of conventional framework.

Meditation in various forms was in fact an ancient Indian practice, but it underwent dramatic transformations as it spread east. Bodhidharma turned it into Zen to meet Chinese requirements, and then Master Linchi in particular turned the tables on tradition:

> Some fill themselves with food and then sit to meditate. They try to catch every delusion before it escapes, they avoid noise, and they seek quiet. This is nothing but deviation from the true way. Didn't the early predecessors tell us that people who seek quiet and try to calm their thoughts are nothing but charlatans?

There is early evidence that some people mistakenly thought meditation only meant sitting quietly. In The Holy Teaching of Vimalakirti, we find Vimalakirti saying to Sariputra, whom he came upon meditating quietly in the forest:

> This is not the way to meditate. Meditation is living in the present without clinging to body or mind. True meditation is being able to retain a calm, detached state no matter what you're doing. Meditation is neither falling into internal quiet nor external diversion. Meditation is entering nirvana without cutting off the passions and behaviors of the world. Those who absorb themselves in these ways are the ones the Lord Buddha would recognize as true meditators.

When meditating, it doesn't matter whether you're sitting or lying down, standing or squatting, or walking or running. In other words, genuine meditating is living without clinging, and without grasping, without trying to rid yourself of anything no matter what you're doing. This is not a rejection of sitting meditation; rather, it is emphasizing that the meditative attitude rather than the position is important. Striving for peace of mind is not the objective; rather, maintaining a pure heart is essential, regardless of what you are doing. Korean Great Master Hyujong Sosan (1520-1604CE), in his "Mirror of Zen," states, "Retaining the pure, original heart is the best way to make progress." He meant that you should neither strive to rid yourself of anything nor soil your heart in any way. Trying to find the right way is not the right way. The object is to unveil your original, pure, undefiled heart.

Early meditation was sitting meditation, so it largely precluded action. But meditation is not only sitting: It is sublimating and integrating mind and action by concentration on everything you do in daily life.

*****

Master Linchi further told his disciples: "You're always talking about practicing and becoming enlightened to the truth. What do you mean by religious truth and how do you practice the Way? What are you lacking in your behavior right now and what are you trying to correct?"

He meant that we should forget words and direct our attention to that which exists before words. Linchi begins with the original, pure mind. Each person is originally a warm, pure, individual form of existence that is absolute. And "original" means "right now."

He spoke again:

"You are fully grown men abiding in tranquility. The problem is that you have no self-confidence. You forget to look for your own face so you spend your time looking at others' faces. But the answer is here, now. Right now."

Well then, what is one's real face? Linchi is saying that we shouldn't be looking for water outside the ocean.

He continued:

"If you want to understand everything, then don't be confused by others. Detach yourself from everything you find within and outside of yourself. If you meet the Buddha kill him. If you meet the predecessors kill them. If you meet holy men kill them, too. Only then will you pass into total freedom."

In other words, you have to detach yourself even from the Buddha, the predecessors, tradition, teachers, and society, everything if you are to achieve total liberation. Linchi rejected everything resolutely. The reason? Because if you let yourself be trapped by any of these, you are depriving yourself of realizing and creating your own unique values and experience. He emphasized freeing yourself from the restrictions of any type of organized religion. Meditation highly regards creativity and totally rejects imitation. Proper understanding, or enlightenment, according to Linchi, is unequivocally pure wisdom and an open Eye.

In general, Zen masters express things radically in order to invoke a true experience because conventional words and sounds are already dead. The only way to use conditioned words effectively is radically and through paradoxes. To "kill" everyone you meet means to detach yourself from them, to conquer them. The use of the word "kill" jolts people into thinking about what they are doing.

*****

Very early Buddhism in India was founded on compassion to overcome suffering and it was concerned with numerous negative aspects of life. In contrast, Zen Buddhism is an unconditional affirmation of the present moment.

Understanding truth through Zen cannot be done through explanations or interpretations. Zen is a method for people to confirm for themselves the truth inside. That is why they say not to look outside the self for answers; something that comes in through the door cannot become the true gem of the inner sanctum. Knowledge and information are no more than transiting dust. It is only through discovering one's innate wisdom that one becomes a real human and can fully express one's real self.

But people nowadays have minds and mouths that run a mile a minute. Their hearts and their feet have now taken the backseat. They no longer feel and they no longer walk. Overly conditioned, abstract-minded people lose their natural liveliness. We are distancing ourselves from the earth. And the earth is the very root of life.

Meditation is training the body and mind in close contact with the earth. Sitting meditation relies on nothing. It is sitting firm and upright, like a mountain. Not to become enlightened. Rather, in itself it is the very form of the original self. It is the easiest Dharma talk of all. *(1985)*

64. The Prison of Plenty

In late spring when wild roses blossom into clouds of white and the cuckoos start to sing their hearts out, the days begin to get drier. But while we have plenty of liquids to quench our own thirst, we tend to overlook the thirsty plants around us. Last evening around sunset, I fetched springwater for the thirsty vegetable patch. By morning, the vegetables had vibrantly come back to life in response to a little concern and care. When the time comes, I'll feel bad about pulling the lettuce, mallow, and crown daisies out of their homes so that I can eat.

This morning I hung up the bamboo blinds. There's a certain elegance to everything when you look out between the thin slits of bamboos. Everything looks more beautiful and secretive when it is partially covered. But today people seem to like to let everything hang out. We have become so feeble inside that we expose the outside. So there's not much left to relish or cherish anymore.

After living in the mountains for a while, a person becomes ignorant of the world and it becomes easy to de-condition your thinking. To get a feel for the world you have to go down to where the action is in order to observe and to get a new perspective on your life in the mountains.

A few days ago I went off to a nearby city to buy some grain and some supplies to fix the earthen chimney. I also bought some tarpaulin to cover the stockpile of rice stalks that I burn for fuel during the rainy season. It was only early June but it already seemed like summer in the city. People were in short sleeves, had their pants rolled up, unabashedly exposed their chests, and wore flimsy see-through clothing.

Little kids, of course, look cool and cute running around like that, but adults look rather cheap when they are dressed, or rather undressed, that way. I'm aware of the trends nowadays toward showing off and exposing more and more, but to walk around in public overly exposed looks both crude and rude. If we aren't covered by as much fur as the beasts, then maybe we should cover up with something. We seem more civil when we can distinguish between what should and shouldn't be exposed.

Amid the clamor and commotion of the bus terminal, I witnessed people who sat transfixed by a television, stiffly and somberly as if at a prayer ceremony. They evidently were the followers of a new Church of Television, the victims of video. Such a scene is not unique to bus terminals. Just go to the local grocery store and watch people immobilized in front of the idiot box. Take a bus and watch the people craning their necks to see some athletic event or a cheap movie. As a form of mass media, the television can be highly educational and informative at times but, when used for the wrong purposes it is nothing more than an enemy of the people, doping them and robbing them of their humanity.

The German philosopher Herbert Marcuse uses the metaphor "prison of plenty"for this era we live in. In the prison there is a refrigerator, a washing machine, a television antenna, and a video. We are all now caught in that prison and we don't even realize it.

The question is how to escape, and it is a question that everyone has to deal with. In order to break out of the dissatisfying, boring routines of everyday life, each of us has to have our own clear discipline. And to establish such discipline, we require not only resistance to laziness but also the ability to make and to break. To grow a tree properly, you have to be able to break off the unnecessary and unsightly branches. In nature the wind does it for the trees. But, as people, we have to do it to ourselves and for ourselves.

The more complicated, frenzied, and fast-paced the world becomes, the more simply we should live. The more we are barraged by outside distractions, the more we should look within. We have to decide what we want to become and what we want to accomplish, instead of letting the proliferation of materialism distract us.

When we live simply our hearts are at peace and we recapture our basic ways. Simple interiors are less costly and less boring. We can also become more devoted to the tasks at hand by simplifying our interpersonal relationships.

We are being controlled by conditioning, by habits, and by the flow of things around us. Here again, rather than looking outside for answers, we should look clearly within in order to change our habits and break out of the flow around us. This requires constant mindfulness and introspection.

In order to achieve a simpler life, you have to discipline yourself. Don't look at what you don't have to, don't read what you don't have to, don't listen to what you don't have to, and don't eat what you don't have to. The less you see, read, listen to, and eat, the better. Your life will be less exhausting and you'll be less worn out as a person. As the old saying goes, less is more.

Happiness cannot be achieved through bigger products and larger quantities. Happiness requires extreme simplicity and plainness. We can find happiness even in the smallest things. We can remain happy regardless of circumstances if we know how to lead a life filled with simple ways and a noble spirit.

Last month on my way back from a trip, I stopped by a relative's home. In less than ten minutes I was exhausted. The conversation, after initial greetings, was halfhearted and we really had nothing to say. Even among close friends, if you don't have some kind of mutual intellectual interest, then the conversation revolves around daily trivia. Everyday activities are kind of a show in themselves, but usually a show without depth, and such conversations can be exhausting.

Nowadays people talk about family crises. Of course there may be many reasons for them, but it seems to me that the main reason is that conversations have been cut short. Family members don't talk anymore. Conversations between people ought to be opportunities to creatively approach life. But even creative efforts, if there is no common interest, naturally get buried in the banalities of everyday life. And when that happens, people lose their vigor for life, their existence becomes merely dutiful, and they become trapped in the prison of plenty.

The greatest implement to be used in breaking out of the prison of plenty is constant awareness. There is no way out without introspection. Only those who are fully awake can lead full lives, and it is those people who can lead relentless escapes from the prison of plenty and improve the quality of life.

A rewarding life is one that is filled with meaning, not one that is filled with the gratification of desires. Without meaning life becomes nothing more than an empty shell. *(1985)*

65. Blinded by the Written Word

There are times when I feel burdened by my books, even though right now I don't have many. I'm aware that many people consider books a very important part of the Path, but when I try to clear out some of the books that I have amassed, I really sense how burdensome they are. Last fall when I was repairing my room, I realized that the reason why I had so many books was that they had come from friends' bookshelves. And recently I've discovered another reason, in addition to the sheer numbers, for my discontent with books: Many of them are filled with worthless dribble that serves only as impediments to the vibrant voices and clear thinking that we need.

I've become skeptical as to the necessity for such a huge amount of information and knowledge. In former times, scholars tried to behave in accordance with their knowledge. They tried to improve their character by integrating their knowledge and their behavior. Consequently, they never betrayed their consciences and they did not just stand by whenever they saw injustice.

But today's scholars and intellectuals immerse themselves in a flood of information and knowledge, resulting in a great imbalance between their knowledge and their behavior. And each time they open their mouths, it's filled with somebody else's latest theory. There is little attempt to bring forth one's own ideas or creativity.

Once when I was wandering about between meditation seasons, the weather was getting nasty so I stayed for a few days at a temple in the south. The temple master was quite elderly but still every morning after homage in the Main Buddha Hall he returned to his own room and without fail recited the Sutra of Complete Enlightenment. I can still vividly remember a certain quote from the sutra: "When your mind is clear, everything you see is clear; when everything you see is clear, then your vision is clear; and when your vision is clear, your perception is clear."

I learned that the monk had recited the sutra every morning for decade after decade. I couldn't help but be moved when, from my room each morning, I heard him reciting.

However, one morning suddenly he stopped chanting and I heard him scream, "You rude little son of a gun, you little snip!" and then from a much crispier, much younger voice, "You old goat! Open your eyes!" I wondered what it was all about so I dashed over to his room.

The master and a young wandering monk who had arrived the day before were sitting face-to-face and shouting. The elderly monk had become so enraged that he had lost his cool completely. But the young monk, with a slight grin on this face, was tapping the old monk on the forehead with his much-treasured copy of the Sutra of Complete Enlightenment.

For decades, the old monk had recited the sutra every morning, yet he had no inkling on how to live the sutra. He expressed the purity of the sutra through his mouth but he was unaware of how to express the purity of his own heart. The young Zen monk refused to become blinded by the printed word and wanted the older monk to read the real sutra, the sutra of his heart. *(1975)*